AMISH-INSPIRED QUILTS

for Today's Home

By Carl Hentsch

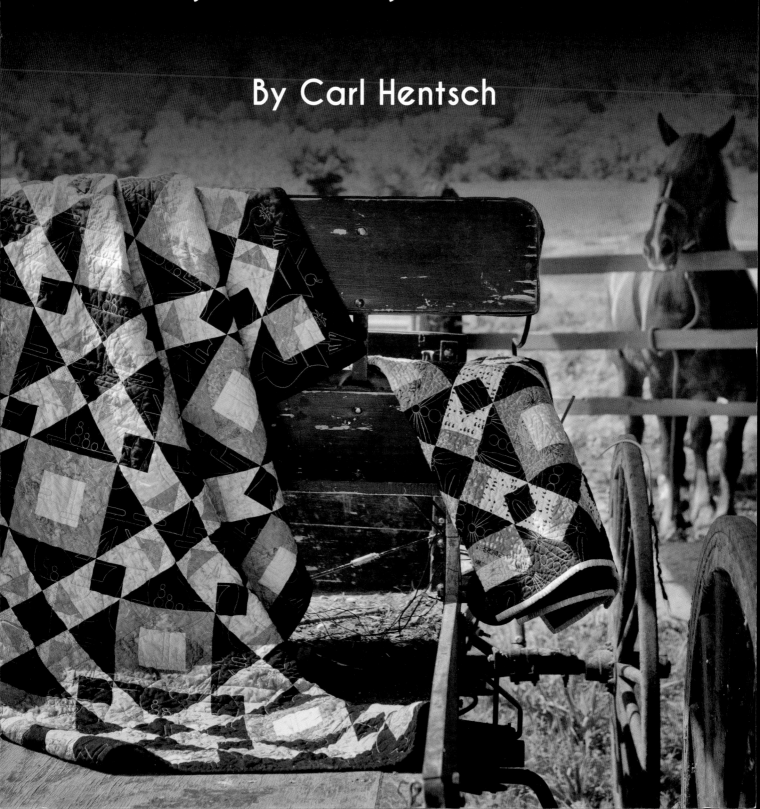

AMISH-INSPIRED QUILTS

for Today's Home

10 Brilliant Patchwork Quilts
By Carl Hentsch

Publisher: **Amy Marson**

Creative Director: **Gailen Runge**

Editor: **Donna di Natale**

Technical Editor: **Jane Miller**

Cover/Book Designer: **Kim Walsh**

Photography: **Aaron T. Leimkuehler**

Illustration: **Eric Sears**

Photo Editor: **Jo Ann Groves**

Published by Kansas City Star Quilts, an imprint of C&T Publishing, Inc., P.O. Box 1456, Lafayette, CA 94549

ISBN: 978-1-61745-320-5

Library of Congress Control Number: 2015948528

Printed in the United States of America

10 9 8 7 6 5 4 3 2 1

Table of Contents

4   Meet the Author
5   Introduction
6   General Piecing Instructions
        Flying Geese
        Y Seams

Projects

10   Square Dance
18   Basket Case
30   Shattered Glass
40   In Full Bloom
48   Sunday Picnic
56   House on the Prairie
62   A Formal Affair
70   A New Barn Raising
78   Sun Catcher
88   Falling Stars

Acknowledgments

Thank you to David Hurd for quilting my quilts and to my pattern testers Jeanne Zyck, Janiece Cline and Barbara Wilkerson. A big thank you to Tula Pink for her continued support and encouragement. I would also like to thank the following companies for their support: Creative Grids, In The Beginning Fabrics, FreeSpirit Fabrics, Windham Fabrics and Moda Fabrics. Also, a big shout-out to my local quilt shops, Harper's Fabric and Quilts in Overland Park, Kansas, and Sarah's Fabrics in Lawrence, Kansas. Finally, I want to thank the people of Jamesport, Missouri, for accommodating us during our photo shoot: Step Back in Time Tours (stepbackintimetours.net), Country Heritage Furniture, H&M Country Store, JAM Wood Products, Oak Ridge Furniture and Sherwood Quilts & Crafts.

Meet the Author

Carl started quilting in the late 1990s. He did not come from a quilting family, but there was always some sort of handwork going on around him. His mother was a seamstress, his aunt knitted and his sister Nancy loved to draw. Carl learned sewing, knitting and patternmaking at an early age, probably around 10 or so.

The Internet was still young when Carl started quilting. "I learned by watching TV shows such as "Simply Quilts," "Quilt in a Day" and "Fons & Porter's Love of Quilting." It was only after seeing guest Ricky Tims on one of those programs that Carl decided it was time to buy a sewing machine, some fabric and learn how to quilt. Fortunately, the rotary cutter and similar tools were available by then. "My first quilt was atrocious. The blocks were not the same size, and there were puckers and folds all over the place."

In 2000, Carl moved to Denver, where he discovered his first quilt shop, block-of-the-month projects and tons of fabric. He dabbled over the years, still watching his favorite TV shows to learn more. It was when he moved to St. Joseph, Missouri, in 2006 that Carl started to delve deeper into his passion for quilting. "I found a lot of quilt shops in Kansas City and participated in a few sampler quilts and blocks of the month." By doing these projects, one block at a time, Carl honed his skills.

Since then, Carl has gained notoriety in the quilting world. He has had many patterns published in a variety of quilt magazines and has worked with fabric companies to design and make quilts for their upcoming lines. In 2011, he was a finalist in the McCall's Quilt Design Star competition, and in 2013, his first book, "Stars and Strips Forever," was released.

I can't remember exactly when I saw my first Amish quilt, but it was probably around the time of the U.S. bicentennial celebrations. That was a time of rediscovery and the beginning of the latest resurgence of quilting. Fast-forward to the late 1990s when I rediscovered my love of antique and Amish quilts. When I started quilting my goal was to make reproduction quilts to honor quilts and quilters from the past. As my quilting skills progressed, I realized this was not what I wanted to do after all. Instead, I wanted to put my own stamp on quilting. While I still desired to honor quilts from the past, I sought to interpret them in my own style.

I have always admired Amish quilts and quilting. In my exploration of the Amish and Amish quilts, I discovered that they have evolved over time, albeit more slowly than quilters and quilting outside the Amish community. During my first visit to an Amish community, I was surprised to learn that even though they do not use electricity, they use propane to power modern appliances. And I was astonished to find a "modern" sewing machine operated by a foot treadle.

In my research of Amish quilts, I discovered there are two meanings that can apply to the term:
• Quilts made by an Amish person, or
• Quilts made using any combination of traditional Amish quilt block patterns and/or fabric.
I refer to this last meaning as "Amish inspired."

This book is not intended to be a historical documentation by any means. Rather, I've taken inspiration from the traditional Amish quilts and updated them for today. My major inspiration was from their use of color. Traditional Amish quilts are made from solid fabrics. But as times have changed, some Amish communities have permitted the use of tone-on-tone fabrics or small-scale prints. Black is typically used in many Amish quilts,

but the variety of colors may depend on where the community is located. I learned that the Pennsylvania Amish tend toward the cooler side of the color wheel, using mainly blues, purples and greens with some red thrown in at times, while the Amish of Indiana tend to the warmer side of the color wheel, utilizing combinations from red-orange to yellow-green.

For the quilts in this book, I chose six colors equally spaced around the color wheel. By varying the tints and shades, I was able to generate a larger color palette.

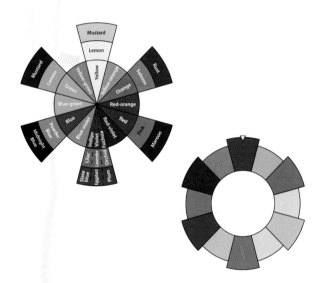

I also didn't limit my projects to just solid fabrics. The first quilt completed, Shattered Glass, is my most "traditional" in that I did use all solids. The other quilts use a combination of print and solid fabrics. When combining prints and solids, I decided to change up where one would typically see these. So in some quilts I used a printed background fabric and solids for the remaining pieces. I also chose to use a variety of small-scale prints and tone-on-tone fabrics.

I hope you enjoy making these Amish-inspired quilts as much as I enjoyed creating them. And remember to honor and respect the quiltmakers who have been creating these beautiful quilts for generations by continuing the tradition.

General Instructions

Flying Geese

For each flying geese unit, you need one large square and four small squares.

1. Draw a line from one corner to the opposite corner on the reverse side of the four small squares.

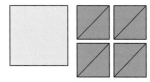

2. Place two small squares on the large square, in opposite corners and right sides together as shown. The lines on the backs of the small squares should flow together as illustrated.

3. Sew two seams, each a scant 1/4" away from the marked lines. Press the unit to set the seams (press flat, as is, do not flip fabrics).

4. Cut the units in half on the drawn lines.

5. Open and press toward the large triangle.

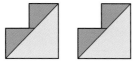

6. Place a small square in the corner of each unit created above, right sides together, with the drawn line positioned as shown.

7. Sew two seams to attach the new square to each unit, each a scant 1/4" away from the marked line – just as you did for the first squares. Press (as is, no lipping) to set the seams.

8. Cut each unit apart on the drawn line (midway between the seams).

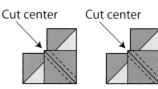

Cut center   Cut center

9. Open and press toward the small triangle to create four flying geese units.

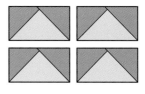

Amish-Inspired
Quilts
for Today's Home

Y Seams

A New Barn Raising and Sun Catcher are made with Y seams. Don't panic.
Y seams are not that difficult if you follow these simple directions.

1. Make a mark 1/4" from the edge on the wrong side of each piece to be joined in the Y seam.

2. Pin the 2 pieces together. Sew the first seam beginning at the first mark and stopping at the second mark. Secure each end with 1 or 2 back stitches. Finger press the seam away from the next piece to be added.

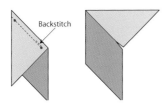

3. Join the next piece, aligning the marks, and pin in place. Stitch as before, starting and stopping at the marks. Make sure that the seam allowances from the previous step are out of the way. Open and finger press the seam allowance again.

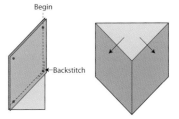

4. Join the next piece as before, aligning the marks, pinning, sewing and finger pressing.

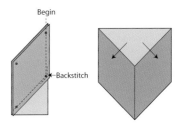

Foundation Piecing

Shattered Glass, on page 31, is made using paper foundation patterns.
The foundation patterns are on page 33-34. Read over these instructions
before copying the patterns to make the quilt.

Amish-Inspired
Quilts
for Today's Home

Square Dance

This is an easy block, just a square in a square set on point. I used a wide sashing unit to set the blocks apart. The squares in the center could easily be cut from a large-scale print or fussy cut from a special fabric. I love this block with the sashing because secondary designs are formed that look like interlocking squares. The quilt makers chose batiks or print fabrics, but I think this quilt would look equally good in solids.

Yardage and Cutting Chart

	Crib 38" x 55"	Lap 55" x 72"	Twin 68" x 85"	Queen 92" x 108"	King 108" x 108"
Black	2 yards	2 7/8 yards	4 3/4 yards	7 1/8 yards	8 1/8 yards
Blocks	(3) 5 3/8" strips cut into (19) 5 3/8" squares; cut each square on the diagonal once to yield (38) D triangles	(6) 5 3/8" strips cut into (41) 5 3/8" squares; cut each square on the diagonal once to yield (82) D triangles	(6) 5 3/8" strips cut into (41) 5 3/8" squares; cut each square on the diagonal once, (82) D triangles	(11) 5 3/8" strips cut into (71) 5 3/8" squares; cut each square on the diagonal once to yield (142) D triangles	(13) 5 3/8" strips cut into (90) 5 3/8" squares; cut each square on the diagonal once to yield (180) D triangles
	(1) 5 3/4" strip cut into (5) 5 3/4" squares; cut each square on the diagonal twice to yield (20) G triangles	(2) 5 3/4" strips cut into (7) 5 3/4" squares; cut each square on the diagonal twice to yield (28) G triangles	(2) 5 3/4" strips cut into (7) 5 3/4" squares; cut each square on the diagonal twice to yield (28) G triangles	(2) 5 3/4" strips cut into (9) 5 3/4" squares; cut each square on the diagonal twice to yield (36) G triangles	(2) 5 3/4" strips cut into (10) 5 3/4" squares; cut each square on the diagonal twice to yield (40) G triangles
Sashing	(1) 5 1/2" strip cut into (3) 5 1/2" squares; cut each square on the diagonal twice to yield (10) Z triangles	(1) 5 1/2" strip cut into (4) 5 1/2" squares; cut each square on the diagonal twice to yield (14) Z triangles	(1) 5 1/2" strip cut into (4) 5 1/2" squares; cut each square on the diagonal twice to yield (14) Z triangles	(1) 5 1/2" strip cut into (5) 5 1/2" squares; cut each square on the diagonal twice to yield (18) Z triangles	(1) 5 1/2" strip cut into (5) 5 1/2" squares; cut each square on the diagonal twice to yield (20) Z triangles
	(2) 4 1/4" strips cut into (12) 4 1/4" L squares	(3) 4 1/4" strips cut into (24) 4 1/4" L squares	(3) 4 1/4" strips cut into (24) 4 1/4" L squares	(5) 4 1/4" strips cut into (40) 4 1/4" L squares	(6) 4 1/4" strips cut into (50) 4 1/4" L squares
	(1) 3 1/2" strip cut into (7) 3 1/2" Y squares	(2) 3 1/2" strips cut into (17) 3 1/2" Y squares	(2) 3 1/2" strips cut into (17) 3 1/2" Y squares	(3) 3 1/2" strips cut into (31) 3 1/2" Y squares	(4) 3 1/2" strips cut into (40) 3 1/2" Y squares
Border	(5) 2 1/2" strips	(7) 2 1/2" strips	(8) 9" strips	(10) 12 1/2" strips	(11) 12 1/2" strips
Binding	(5) 2 1/4" strips	(7) 2 1/4" strips	(7) 2 1/4" strips	(8) 2 1/4" strips	(12) 2 1/4" strips
Orange	5/8 yard	1 yard	1 yard	1 3/4 yards	2 1/8 yards
Blocks	(2) 5 3/4" strips cut into (12) 5	(4) 5 3/4" strips cut into (24) 5	(4) 5 3/4" strips cut into (24) 5	(7) 5 3/4" strips cut into (40) 5	(9) 5 3/4" strips cut into (50) 5

	3/4" squares; cut each square on the diagonal twice to yield (48) C triangles	3/4" squares; cut each square on the diagonal twice to yield (96) C triangles	3/4" squares; cut each square on the diagonal twice to yield (96) C triangles	3/4" squares; cut each square on the diagonal twice to yield (160) C triangles	3/4" squares; cut each square on the diagonal twice to yield (200) C triangles
Sashing	(2) 4 1/4" strips cut into (12) 4 1/4" L squares	(3) 4 1/4" strips cut into (24) 4 1/4" L squares	(3) 4 1/4" strips cut into (24) 4 1/4" L squares	(5) 4 1/4" strips cut into (40) 4 1/4" L squares	(6) 4 1/4" strips cut into (50) 4 1/4" L squares
Dark Gray	**1/3 yard**	**1/2 yard**	**1/2 yard**	**2/3 yard**	**7/8 yard**
Blocks	(2) 3 1/8" strips cut into (19) 3 1/8" squares; cut each square on the diagonal once to yield (38) B triangles	(4) 3 1/8" strips cut into (41) 3 1/8" B squares; cut each square on the diagonal once to yield (82) B triangles	(4) 3 1/8" strips cut into (41) 3 1/8"B squares; cut each square on the diagonal once to yield (82) B triangles	(6) 3 1/8" strips cut into (71) 3 1/8" B squares; cut each square on the diagonal once to yield (142) B triangles	(8) 3 1/8" strips cut into (90) 3 1/8" B squares; cut each square on the diagonal once to yield (180) B triangles
	(1) 3 1/2" strip cut into (5) 3 1/2" squares; cut each square on the diagonal twice to yield (20) F triangles	(1) 3 1/2" strip cut into (7) 3 1/2" squares; cut each square on the diagonal twice to yield (28) F triangles	(1) 3 1/2" strip cut into (7) 3 1/2" squares; cut each square on the diagonal twice to yield (28) F triangles	(1) 3 1/2" strip cut into (9) 3 1/2" squares; cut each square on the diagonal twice to yield (36) F triangles	(1) 3 1/2" strip cut into (10) 3 1/2" squares; cut each square on the diagonal twice to yield (40) F triangles
Medium Gray	**1/4 yard**	**1/2 yard**	**1/2 yard**	**3/4 yard**	**1 yard**
Sashing	(3) 2 3/8" strips cut into (48) 2 3/8" M squares	(6) 2 3/8" strips cut into (96) 2 3/8" M squares	(6) 2 3/8" strips cut into (96) 2 3/8" M squares	(10) 2 3/8" strips cut into (160) 2 3/8" M squares	(13) 2 3/8" strips cut into (200) 2 3/8" M squares
Yellow	**1/3 yard**	**3/8 yard**	**3/8 yard**	**1/2 yard**	**5/8 yard**
Block	(2) 3 5/8" strips cut into (8) 3 5/8" A squares (6) 2 1/8" x 3 5/8" E rectangles	(3) 3 5/8" strips cut into (18) 3 5/8" A squares (10) 2 1/8" x 3 5/8" E rectangles	(3) 3 5/8" strips cut into (18) 3 5/8" A squares (10) 2 1/8" x 3 5/8" E rectangles	(4) 3 5/8" strips cut into (32) 3 5/8" A squares (14) 2 1/8" x 3 5/8" E rectangles	(5) 3 5/8" strips cut into (41) 3 5/8" A squares (16) 2 1/8" x 3 5/8" E rectangles
	(1) 2 1/8" strip cut into (4) 2 1/8" H squares	(1) 2 1/8" strip cut into (4) 2 1/8" H squares	(1) 2 1/8" strip cut into (4) 2 1/8" H squares	(1) 2 1/8" strip cut into (4) 2 1/8" H squares	(1) 2 1/8" strip cut into (4) 2 1/8" H squares
Green	**5/8 yard**	**1 yard**	**1 yard**	**1 5/8 yards**	**2 yards**
Sashing	(3) 3 1/2" strips cut into (48) 2" x 3 1/2" N rectangles	(5) 3 1/2" strips cut into (96) 2" x 3 1/2" N rectangles	(5) 3 1/2" strips cut into (96) 2" x 3 1/2" N rectangles	(8) 3 1/2" strips cut into (160) 2" x 3 1/2" N rectangles	(10) 3 1/2" strips cut into (200) 2" x 3 1/2" N rectangles
	(3) 2 3/8" strips cut into (48) 2 3/8" M squares	(6) 2 3/8" strips cut into (96) 2 3/8" M squares	(6) 2 3/8" strips cut into (96) 2 3/8" M squares	(10) 2 3/8" strips cut into (160) 2 3/8" M squares	(12) 2 3/8" strips cut into (200) 2 3/8" M squares
				squares	
Backing	**2 5/8 yards**	**3 3/4 yards**	**5 1/2 yards**	**8 2/3 yards**	**10 yards**

Block Assembly (9" square finished)

Quilt Size	Crib	Lap	Twin	Queen	King
Blocks required	8	18	18	32	41
Side Setting Triangles	6	10	10	14	16
Corner Triangles	4	4	4	4	4

Using the illustrations as your guide, assemble the number of blocks required for your quilt size.

Each block is made up of (1) A square, (4) B triangles, (4) C triangles and (4) D triangles.

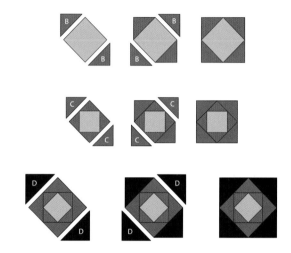

Side Setting Triangles

Following the illustrations, assemble the required number of setting triangles.

Each setting triangle is made up of

(1) E rectangle, (1) B triangle, (2) F triangles, (2) C triangles, (1) D triangle and (2) G triangles.

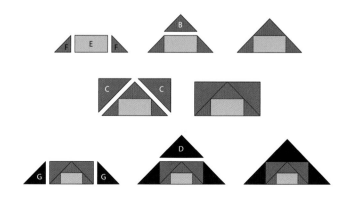

By Carl Hentsch

Corner Triangles

Following the illustrations, make (4) corner triangles.

Each corner triangle is made up of
(1) C triangle, **(2)** F triangles, **(2)** G triangles and **(1)** H square.

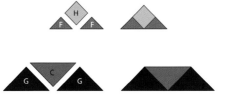

~~~~~~

Flying Geese

Follow the General Piecing directions for making flying geese units on page 6.

Flying Geese Units	Crib	Lap	Twin	Queen	King
Orange / Medium Gray	48	96	96	160	200
Black / Green	48	96	96	160	200

1. To make four flying geese units, you will need:
(1) Orange L square, (4) Medium Gray M squares, (1) Black L square and (4) Green M squares

2. Assemble the sashing units as shown using
(2) green N rectangles, (2) orange/medium gray flying geese and (2) black/green flying geese.
Make the number of sashing units required.

Amish-Inspired
Quilts
for Today's Home

Quilt Top Assembly

1. Lay out your quilt in diagonal rows as shown. Place the Y squares in between the sashing units and the Z triangles at the ends (a.k.a., mini setting triangles).

2. Measure your quilt from top to bottom. Cut the side borders to length and attach to your quilt. Be sure to check the chart for the correct width of the border strips

3. Measure your quilt from side to side. Cut the top and bottom borders to length and attach to your quilt.

Crib Layout Guide

By Carl Hentsch

Crib   Lap/Twin   Queen   King

Layout Guide for All Sizes

Amish-Inspired
Quilts
for Today's Home

Lap Size Quilt

By Carl Hentsch

Amish-Inspired
Quilts
for Today's Home

Basket Case

I have always loved the traditional basket block. Because it is typically set on point, I thought it was a good fit for a diagonal set quilt. I wanted the larger quilts to be quick, so I added a lot of negative space. Great for quilting and fewer blocks to piece. I used a unique setting so the blocks appear to be floating on a sea of gray. The king-size quilt is my homage to the traditional Center Diamond Quilt.

Yardage and Cutting Chart

	Crib 38" x 55"	Lap 55" x 72"	Full 72" x 90"	Queen 92" x 108"	King 108" x 108"
Gray	**2 1/2 yards**	**3 2/3 yards**	**5 3/4 yards**	**8 3/4 yards**	**9 3/4 yards**
Blocks	(3) 3 1/2" strips cut into (20) 3 1/2" squares; cut each square on the diagonal once to yield (40) A triangles	(4) 3 1/2" strips cut into (45) 3 1/2" squares; cut each square on the diagonal once to yield (90) A triangles	(5) 3 1/2" strips cut into (48) 3 1/2" squares; cut each square on the diagonal once to yield (95) A triangles	(5) 3 1/2" strips cut into (50) 3 1/2" squares; cut each square on the diagonal once to yield (100) A triangles	(5) 3 1/2" strips cut into (53) 3 1/2" squares; cut each square on the diagonal once to yield (105) A triangles
	(4) 1 7/8" strips cut into (16) 7 1/4" x 1 7/8" B rectangles	(8) 1 7/8" strips cut into (36) 7 1/4" x 1 7/8" B rectangles	(8) 1 7/8" strips cut into (38) 7 1/4" x 1 7/8" B rectangles	(8) 1 7/8" strips cut into (40) 7 1/4" x 1 7/8" B rectangles	(9) 1 7/8" strips cut into (42) 7 1/4" x 1 7/8" B rectangles
	(2) 2 3/4" strips cut into (16) 2 3/4" squares; cut each square on the diagonal once to yield (32) C triangles	(3) 2 3/4" strips cut into (36) 2 3/4" squares; cut each square on the diagonal once to yield (72) C triangles	(3) 2 3/4" strips cut into (38) 2 3/4" squares; cut each square on the diagonal once to yield (76) C triangles	(3) 2 3/4" strips cut into (40) 2 3/4" squares; cut each square on the diagonal once to yield (80) C triangles	(3) 2 3/4" strips cut into (42) 2 3/4" squares; cut each square on the diagonal once to yield (84) C triangles
			(1) 9 1/2" strip cut into (4) 9 1/2" squares	(8) 9 1/2" strips cut into (30) 9 1/2" squares	(10) 9 1/2" strips cut into (40) 9 1/2" squares
Sashing	(4) 3 1/2" strips cut into (4) 9 1/2" x 3 1/2" Q rectangles, (12) 8" x 3 1/2" P rectangles and (7) 3 1/2" Y squares	(7) 3 1/2" strips cut into (4) 9 1/2" x 3 1/2" Q rectangles, (20) 8" x 3 1/2" P rectangles and (17) 3 1/2" Y squares	(9) 3 1/2" strips cut into (4) 9 1/2" x 3 1/2" Q rectangles, (24) 8" x 3 1/2" P rectangles, (8) 6 1/2" x 3 1/2" R rectangles and (22) 3 1/2" Y squares	(18) 3 1/2" strips cut into (4) 9 1/2" x 3 1/2" Q rectangles, (36) 8" x 3 1/2" P rectangles, (32) 6 1/2" x 3 1/2" R rectangles and (49) 3 1/2" Y squares	(22) 3 1/2" strips cut into (4) 9 1/2" x 3 1/2" Q rectangles, (40) 8" x 3 1/2" P rectangles, (48) 6 1/2" x 3 1/2" R rectangles and (60) 3 1/2" Y squares
	(1) 4 1/4" strip	(2) 4 1/4" strip	(2) 4 1/4" strips	(6) 4 1/4" strips	(7) 4 1/4" strips

	cut into (7) 4 1/4" L squares	cut into (17) 4 1/4" L squares	cut into (17) 4 1/4" L squares	cut into (49) 4 1/4" L squares	cut into (60) 4 1/4" L squares
Large Setting Triangles	(1) 14" strip cut into (2) 13 7/8" squares; cut each square on the diagonal twice to yield (6) setting triangles	(2) 14" strips cut into (3) 13 7/8" squares; cut each square on the diagonal twice to yield (10) setting triangles	(2) 14" strips cut into (3) 13 7/8" squares; cut each square on the diagonal twice to yield (12) setting triangles	(3) 14" strips cut into (5) 13 7/8" squares; cut each square on the diagonal twice to yield (18) setting triangles	(3) 14" strips cut into (5) 13 7/8" squares; cut each square on the diagonal twice to yield (20) setting triangles
Mini Setting Triangles	(1) 5 1/2" strips cut into (3) 5 1/2" squares; cut each square on the diagonal twice to yield (10) Z triangles	(1) 5 1/2" strip cut into (4) 5 1/2" squares; cut each square on the diagonal twice to yield (14) Z triangles	(1) 5 1/2" strip cut into (4) 5 1/2" squares; cut each square on the diagonal twice to yield (16) Z triangles	(1) 5 1/2" strip cut into (6) 5 1/2" squares; cut each square on the diagonal twice to yield (22) Z triangles	(1) 5 1/2" strip cut into (6) 5 1/2" squares; cut each square on the diagonal twice to yield (24) Z triangles
Corner Triangle	(1) 7 1/4" strip cut into (2) 7 1/4" squares; Cut each square on the diagonal once to yield (4) corner triangles	(1) 7 1/4" strip cut into (2) 7 1/4" squares; Cut each square on the diagonal once to yield (4) corner triangles	(1) 7 1/4" strip cut into (2) 7 1/4" squares; Cut each square on the diagonal once to yield (4) corner triangles	(1) 7 1/4" strip cut into (2) 7 1/4" squares; Cut each square on the diagonal once to yield (4) corner triangles	(1) 7 1/4" strip cut into (2) 7 1/4" squares; Cut each square on the diagonal once to yield (4) corner triangles
Borders	(5) 2 1/2" strips	(7) 2 1/2" strips	(5) 11 1/2" strips (sides) (4) 3 1/2" strips (top & bottom)	(11) 3 3/4" strips	(12) 3 1/2" strips
Dusty Rose	**5/8 yard**	**1 yard**	**1 1/4 yard**	**1 3/4 yards**	**2 yards**
Sashing	(1) 3 1/2" strip cut into (16) 2" x 3 1/2" N rectangles	(3) 3 1/2" strips cut into (48) 2" x 3 1/2" N rectangles	(3) 3 1/2" strips cut into (48) 2" x 3 1/2" N rectangles	(5) 3 1/2" strips cut into (96) 2" x 3 1/2" N rectangles	(6) 3 1/2" strips cut into (104) 2" x 3 1/2" N rectangles
	(1) 2 3/8" strip; cut into (16) 2 3/8" M squares	(3) 2 3/8" strip; cut into (48) 2 3/8" M squares	(3) 2 3/8" strip; cut into (48) 2 3/8" M squares	(6) 2 3/8" strips; cut into (96) 2 3/8" M squares	(7) 2 3/8" strips; cut into (104) 2 3/8" M squares
Binding	(5) 2 1/4" strips	(7) 2 1/4" strips	(9) 2 1/4" strips	(11) 2 1/4" strips	(12) 2 1/4" strips
Teal	**1/2 yard**	**7/8 yard**	**1 yard**	**1 1/2 yards**	**1 7/8 yards**
Blocks	(1) 7 1/4" strip cut into (4) 7 1/4" squares; cut each square on the diagonal once to yield (8) D triangles	(2) 7 1/4" strips cut into (9) 7 1/4" squares; cut each square on the diagonal once to yield (18) D triangles	(2) 7 1/4" strips cut into (10) 7 1/4" squares; cut each square on the diagonal once to yield (19) D triangles	(2) 7 1/4" strips cut into (10) 7 1/4" squares; cut each square on the diagonal once to yield (20) D triangles	(3) 7 1/4" strips cut into (11) 7 1/4" squares; cut each square on the diagonal once to yield (21) D triangles
	(1) 2 1/8" strip	(1) 2 1/8" strip	(2) 2 1/8" strips	(2) 2 1/8" strips	(2) 2 1/8" strips

Amish-Inspired
Quilts
for Today's Home

	cut into (8) 2 1/8" squares; cut each square on the diagonal once to yield (16) E triangles	cut into (18) 2 1/8" squares; cut each square on the diagonal once to yield (36) E triangles	cut into (19) 2 1/8" squares; cut each square on the diagonal once (38) E triangles	cut into (20) 2 1/8" squares; cut each square on the diagonal once to yield (38) E triangles	cut into (21) 2 1/8" squares; cut each square on the diagonal once to yield (42) E triangles
Sashing	(2) 2 3/8" strips cut into (28) 2 3/8" M squares	(5) 2 3/8" strips cut into (68) 2 3/8" M squares	(6) 2 3/8" strips cut into (88) 2 3/8" M squares	(13) 2 3/8" strips cut into (196) 2 3/8" M squares	(15) 2 3/8" strips cut into (240) 2 3/8" M squares
Gold	1/8 yard	1/4 yard	1/4 yard	3/8 yard	3/8 yard
Sashing	(1) 4 1/4" strip cut into (4) 4 1/4"L squares	(2) 4 1/4" strips cut into (12) 4 1/4" L squares	(2) 4 1/4" strips cut into (12) 4 1/4" L squares	(3) 4 1/4" strips cut into (24) 4 1/4" L squares	(3) 4 1/4" strips cut into (26) 4 1/4" L squares
Diamonds	**1 Fat Quarter Each**	**1 Fat Quarter Each**	**1 Fat Quarter Each**	**1 Fat Quarter Each**	**1 Fat Quarter Each**
Dark Blue	(4) 1 3/8" x 22" strips	(8) 1 3/8" x 22" strips	(9) 1 3/8" x 22" strips	(9) 1 3/8" x 22" strips	(10) 1 3/8" x 22" strips
Light Green	(2) 1 3/8" x 22" strips	(4) 1 3/8" x 22" strips	(5) 1 3/8" x 22" strips	(5) 1 3/8" x 22" strips	(5) 1 3/8" x 22" strips
Dark Green	(2) 1 3/8" x 22" strips	(4) 1 3/8" x 22" strips	(5) 1 3/8" x 22" strips	(5) 1 3/8" x 22" strips	(5) 1 3/8" x 22" strips
Light Purple	(2) 1 3/8" x 22" strips	(4) 1 3/8" x 22" strips	(5) 1 3/8" x 22" strips	(5) 1 3/8" x 22" strips	(5) 1 3/8" x 22" strips
Dark Purple	(2) 1 3/8" x 22" strips	(4) 1 3/8" x 22" strips	(5) 1 3/8" x 22" strips	(5) 1 3/8" x 22" strips	(5) 1 3/8" x 22" strips
Light Violet	(2) 1 3/8" x 22" strips	(4) 1 3/8" x 22" strips	(5) 1 3/8" x 22" strips	(5) 1 3/8" x 22" strips	(5) 1 3/8" x 22" strips
Dark Violet	(2) 1 3/8" x 22" strips	(4) 1 3/8" x 22" strips	(5) 1 3/8" x 22" strips	(5) 1 3/8" x 22" strips	(5) 1 3/8" x 22" strips
Backing	3	3 3/4 yards	5 2/3 yards	8 2/3 yards	10 yards

Block Assembly (9" square finished)

Block type	Crib	Lap	Full	Queen	King
Basket Blocks required for quilt	8	18	19	20	21
Plain Blocks required for quilt	0	0	4	30	40

Pieced Diamonds

1. Sew your 1 3/8" x 22" strips into the following pairs. You will need two sets of each pair. Offset the strips by 1" and press the seams in opposite directions.

   a. Light Green/Light Violet

   b. Dark Violet/Dark Blue

   c. Dark Green/Dark Purple

   d. Light Purple/Dark Blue

2. Place a matching pair with rights sides together. Sew together along the long edge and press open.

3. Align the 45-degree line on your ruler with the edge of the fabric or along one of the seam lines. Using a rotary cutter, trim off the end of the fabric.

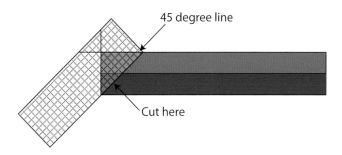

45 degree line

Cut here

4. Find the 1 3/8" line on your rotary ruler. Match the line with the angled left edge of the fabric and align the 45-degree line again.

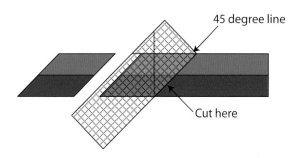

45 degree line

Cut here

5. Cut along the ruler to cut your first shape. Continue cutting 16 diamond pairs from each strip.

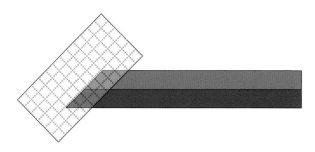

6. Join the strips together to make a diamond unit for each block.

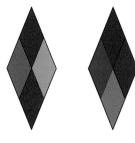

Amish-Inspired Quilts

for Today's Home

Basket Block

Each block requires

(4) diamond units,

(4) A triangles and (4) C triangles.

1. Attach a C triangle to a diamond unit to make a **left corner**. Make 2 using different colored diamond units.

2. Add an A triangle to the right side of each left corner to make a **Unit 1**.

3. Attach a C triangle to a diamond unit to make a **right corner**. Make two, using different colored diamond units.

4. Add an A triangle to the left side of each right corner to make a **Unit 2**. Sew a left corner unit and a right corner unit.

5. Sew together to make a pieced triangle. Make 2.

6. Sew two pieced triangle units together to make a Unit 3.

By Carl Hentsch

Assemble the Basket Blocks

1. Place **(2)** B rectangles wrong sides together. Align the 45-degree line of your ruler along the edge of the strip as shown below and trim the end of the rectangle. You will end up with mirror-image pieces.

2. Sew an E triangle to the squared end of the units created in Step 1. Pay attention to the angle of the triangle.

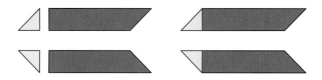

3. Sew the units created in Step 2 to each side of a D triangle. Then sew an A triangle to the bottom.

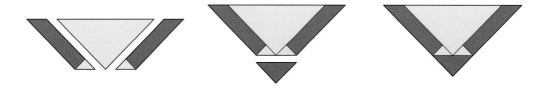

4. Sew the top and bottom halves together to complete your basket block. Make the required number of blocks for your quilt.

Amish-Inspired
Quilts
for Today's Home

Flying Geese

To make four flying geese units (FG) you will need: (1) gray L square and (4) teal M squares; (1) gray L square and (4) dusty rose M squares; and (1) gold L square and (4) teal M squares."

Flying Geese Units	Crib	Lap	Full	Queen	King
Gold/Teal	16	48	48	96	104
Gray/Dusty Rose	16	48	48	96	104
Gray/Teal	12	20	40	100	136

Sashing (3" x 9" Finished)

Sashing Units	Crib	Lap	Full	Queen	King
Plain Sashing	4	4	4	4	4
Sashing 1	8	24	24	48	52
Sashing 2	12	20	24	36	40
Sashing 3	0	0	8	32	48

Referring to the layout guide, assemble the sashing units using the following pieces:

Plain Sashing

Sashing 1

Sashing 2

Gray Y Square

Sashing 3

Sashing 2 Reverse

By Carl Hentsch

25

Quilt Top Assembly

1. Lay out your quilt in diagonal rows as shown. Place the Y squares in between the sashing units and the Z triangles (mini setting triangles) at the ends.

2. Measure your quilt through the center from top to bottom. Cut the side borders to length and attach to your quilt.

3. Now measure your quilt through the center from side to side. Once again, cut the borders to length and attach to your quilt.

King Size Quilt

**Amish-Inspired
Quilts**
for Today's Home

Basket Case Lap

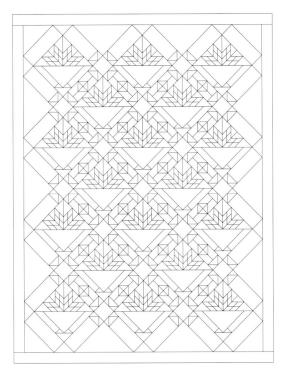

Overall Size: 55.41 by 72.38 inches

Basket Case Full

Overall Size: 72.91 by 90.85 inches

Basket Case Crib

Overall Size: 37.94 by 54.91 inches

Basket Case Queen

Overall Size: 91.35 by 108.32 inches

By Carl Hentsch

Crib Size Quilt

Amish-Inspired
Quilts
for Today's Home

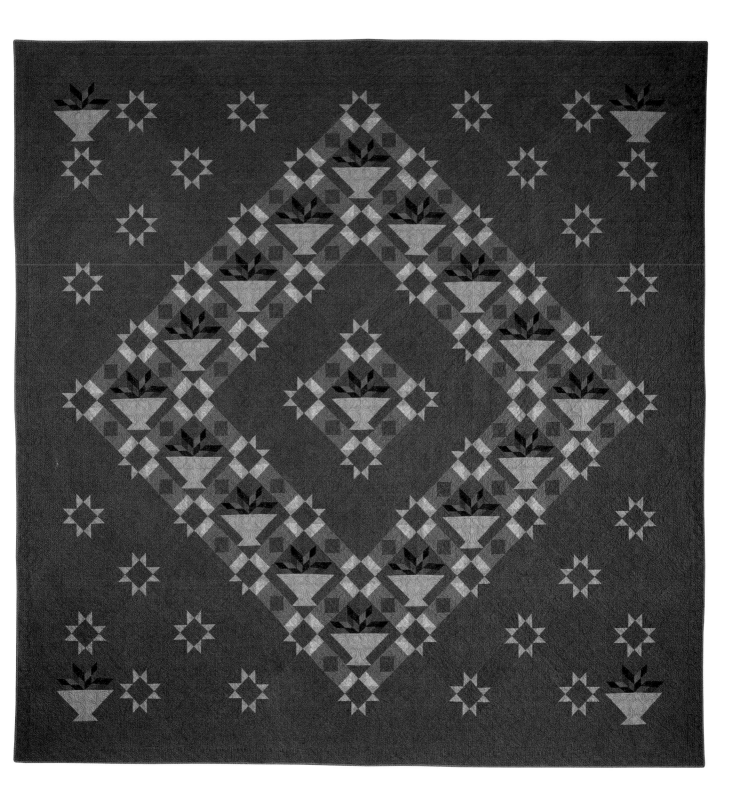

King Size Quilt

By Carl Hentsch

Amish-Inspired
Quilts
for Today's Home

Shattered Glass

I love foundation or paper piecing. It gives me the opportunity to create a more difficult block. This block and quilt were actually the first I designed for this book. The blocks were inspired by the many old barns that I pass every day, with broken windows and walls falling in all around. This is also where I took my idea for the wide sashing units that are incorporated into many of these quilts. This quilt is set in horizontal rows. The largest size for this quilt is a twin, because I quickly realized that I didn't want to piece any more foundations than that and thought other quilt makers would feel the same.

Cutting instructions are for cutting the pieces to be sewn to the foundation papers. I recommend you read through all the instructions before starting to cut or sew.

Yardage and Cutting Chart

	Crib 45" x 57"	Lap 57" x 69"	Twin 69" x 81"
# of Blocks	12	20	30
Black	**3 7/8 yards**	**5 3/4 yards**	**8 yards**
Blocks	Cut (10) 3" strips. Cut each strip into (48) 3" x 6" 60-degree diamonds. Cut each square on the long diagonal into (48) A2 pieces and (48) B2 pieces	Cut (16) 3" strips. Cut each strip into (80) 3" x 6" 60-degree diamonds. Cut each square on the long diagonal into (80) A2 pieces and (80) B2 pieces	Cut (24) 3" strips. Cut each strip into (120) 3" x 6" 60-degree diamonds. Cut each square on the long diagonal into (120) A2 pieces and (120) B2 pieces
	Cut (10) 2 1/2" strips. Cut each strip into (48) A3 and (48) B3 2 1/2" 45-degree diamonds	Cut (16) 2 1/2" strips. Cut each strip into (80) A3 and (80) B3 2 1/2" 45-degree diamonds	Cut (24) 2 1/2" strips. Cut each strip into (120) A3 and (120) B3 2 1/2" 45-degree diamonds
	Cut (8) 3" strips. Cut each strip into (48) 3" x 6" rectangles. Cut each rectangle on the diagonal once to yield (48) A5 pieces and (48) B5 pieces.	Cut (14) 3" strips. Cut each strip into (80) 3" x 6" rectangles. Cut each rectangle on the diagonal once to yield (80) A5 pieces and (80) B5 pieces.	Cut (20) 3" strips. Cut each strip into (48) 3" x 6" rectangles. Cut each rectangle on the diagonal once to yield (120) A5 pieces and (120) B5 pieces
Sashing	Cut (3) 4 1/4" strips. Cut each strip into (21) 4 1/4" L squares	Cut (4) 4 1/4" strips. Cut each strip into (31) 4 1/4" L squares	Cut (5) 4 1/4" strips. Cut each strip each strip into (43) 4 1/4" L squares
Border	Cut (8) 3 1/2" strips. Cut each strip each strip into (24) 3 1/2" Y squares, (18) 3 1/2" x 2" N rectangles and (14) 3 1/2" x 9 1/2" rectangles	Cut (11) 3 1/2" strips. Cut each strip into (34) 3 1/2" Y squares, (22) 3 1/2" x 2" N rectangles and (18) 3 1/2" x 9 1/2" rectangles	Cut (13) 3 1/2" strips. Cut each strip into (46) 3 1/2" Y squares, (26) 3 1/2" x 2" N rectangles and (22) 3 1/2" x 9 1/2" rectangles

By Carl Hentsch

Binding	Cut (6) 2 1/4" strips	Cut (7) 2 1/4" strips	Cut (8) 2 1/4" strips
Yellow	5/8 yard	1 yard	1 1/4 yards
Blocks	Cut (4) 4 1/4" strips. Cut each strip into (48) 4 1/4" x 1 1/2" A1 rectangles and (48) 4 1/4" x 1 1/2" B1 rectangles	Cut (7) 4 1/4" strips. Cut each strip into (80) 4 1/4" 1 1/2" A1 rectangles and (80) 4 1/4" 1 1/2" B1 rectangles	Cut (10) 4 1/4" strips. Cut each strip each strip into (120) 4 1/4" 1 1/2" A1 rectangles and (120) 4 1/4" 1 1/2" B1 rectangles
Purple	1 yard	1 3/8 yard	2 1/8 yards
Blocks	Cut (10) 3" strips. Cut each strip into (48) 3" x 6" 60-degree diamonds. Cut each diamond on the long diagonal once to yield (48) A4 pieces and (48) B4 pieces	Cut (16) 3" strips. Cut each strip into (80) 3" x 6" 60-degree diamonds. Cut each diamond on the long diagonal once to yield (80) A4 pieces and (80) B4 pieces	Cut (24) 3" strips. Cut each strip into (120) 3" x 6" 60-degree diamonds. Cut each diamond on the long diagonal once to yield (120) A4 pieces and (120) B6 pieces
Violet	3/4 yards	1 yard	1 1/2 yards
Sashing	Cut (4) 2 3/8" strips. Cut each strip into (64) 2 3/8" M squares	Cut (7) 2 3/8" strips. Cut each strip into (100) 2 3/8" M squares	Cut (9) 2 3/8" strips. Cut each strip into (144) 2 3/8" M squares
	Cut (4) 3 1/2" strips. Cut each strip into (62) 3 1/2" x 2" N rectangles	Cut (5) 3 1/2" strips. Cut each strip into (98) 3 1/2" x 2" N rectangles	Cut (8) 3 1/2" strips. Cut each strip into (142) 3 1/2" x 2" N rectangles
Blue	1/2 yard	5/8 yard	7/8 yard
Sashing	Cut (6) 2 3/8" strips. Cut each strip into (84) 2 3/8" M squares	Cut (8) 2 3/8" strips. Cut each strip into (124) 2 3/8" M squares	Cut (1) 2 3/8" strips. Cut this strip into (72) 2 3/8" M squares
Orange	3/8 yard	1/2 yard	5/8 yard
Sashing	Cut (2) 4 1/4" strips. Cut each strip each strip into (16) 4 1/4" L squares	Cut (3) 4 1/4" strips. Cut each strip into (25) 4 1/4" L squares	Cut (4) 4 1/4" strips. Cut each strip into (36) 4 1/4" L squares
Backing	3 yards	4 yards	5 yards

Recommended Tools

- ✔ Glue stick or flat head pins

- ✔ Carol Doak's Foundation paper or any other type of paper designed for foundation piecing

- ✔ Add-A-Quarter Ruler

- ✔ Index card, post card or template plastic (to aid in using the add a quarter ruler)

- ✔ Transparent tape (this will mend the foundation if you need to rip out stitches)

Cutting 60-degree Diamonds

1. Place two 3" strips on the cutting mat, wrong sides together.

2. Align the 60-degree line on your ruler with the edge of the fabric. Trim off the end of the fabric as shown in the illustration.

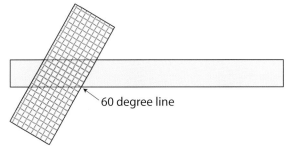

60 degree line

3. Find the 6" line on your ruler. Match the line with the angled left edge of the fabric and align the 60-degree line again.

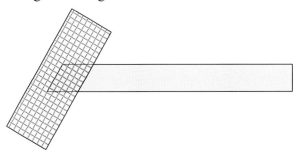

4. Cut along the ruler to make a pair of diamonds. Continue cutting the required number of diamonds for your quilt. Each pair will give you one A and one B piece.

5. To cut the A4 pieces, align the ruler between the points along the long diagonal of the diamond and cut.

Cutting 45-degree Diamonds

The 45-degree diamonds are made in the same manner as the 60-degree diamonds, EXCEPT you align the 45-degree line on the ruler with the edge of the fabric.

Assemble the Blocks
9" finished block

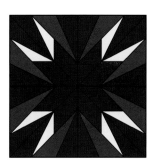

The foundation template is on page 36. You will need to photocopy four paper foundation patterns for each block. To determine how many patterns to copy, multiply the number of blocks in the quilt by four. Cut the foundations from the paper, leaving at least 1/4" of extra space around the outer seam allowance.

1. Place the first fabric right side up on the unprinted side of the foundation, centered on the A1 position and ensuring that you have adequate seam allowance around the entire piece. Pin or use a small amount of glue to secure the fabric in place.

2. Place the foundation with the printed side up on your rotary cutting mat. Place the index card along the sewing line between the A1 and A2 sections and fold the foundation paper back over the card. Place the Add-A-Quarter ruler on the foundation so that the lip of the ruler is pressed up against the crease and the index card.

3. Trim the excess fabric along the ruler edge with your rotary cutter.

4. Fold the foundation back in place and flip over. Place the fabric for A2 face down along the edge you just trimmed on fabric A1. Check to ensure that when you press open A2, it will completely cover the section with adequate seam allowance on all sides.

5. Pin or hold fabric A2 in place and flip the foundation so the printed side is up. Shorten your stitch length to 15-20 stitches per inch and sew on the solid line between sections A1 and A2.

Note: Do not extend your stitching more than 2 or 3 stitches past the printed line.

By Carl Hentsch

6. Cut the thread and press fabric A2 open. Do not use steam as this will weaken your foundation paper.

7. Turn the foundation over so the printed side is up. Place the index card on the line between sections A2 and A3. Fold the foundation as before and use the Add-A-Quarter ruler to trim your seam allowance to 1/4".

8. Place the fabric for section A3 along the trimmed edge of fabric A2, right sides together. Once again, check to make sure the fabric will cover the entire A3 section when pressed. Flip the foundation over and sew on the line between sections A2 and A3.

9. Continue in this manner until the entire section is complete. Now trim the foundation 1/4" from the outer solid line. **DO NOT Cut each square on the line.** Cut 1/4" away from the line for your seam allowance.

10. Complete the above steps with section B.

11. Sew section A and B together.

Make the number of blocks required for the size quilt you have chosen.

 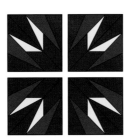 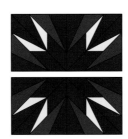 

**Amish-Inspired
Quilts**
for Today's Home

Assemble the Sashing
Flying Geese Sashing Units
3" x 9" finished

To make four flying geese you will need **(1)** Orange L square, **(4)** Blue M squares, **(1)** Black L square and **(4)** Violet M squares. Follow the instructions for making flying geese units on page 6.

For each flying geese sashing unit you will need:

(1) Orange/Blue flying geese **(2)** Black/Violet flying geese **(2)** Violet N rectangles

Make the number of flying geese sashing units required for the size quilt you have chosen.

Crib: 31 units	Lap: 49 units	Twin: 71 units

~~~~~~

Border
The border is made of mini flying geese units and 3 1/2" x 2" N rectangles.

Mini Flying Geese Units

1. To make four mini flying geese units you will need
(1) Black L square and **(4)** Blue M squares.

Follow the instructions on page 6 for making flying geese.

2. Add an N rectangle to each mini flying geese unit. The unit should measure 3 1/2" square.

Make the number of mini flying geese units required for the size quilt you have chosen.

Crib: 18 units	Lap: 22 units	Twin: 26 units

By Carl Hentsch

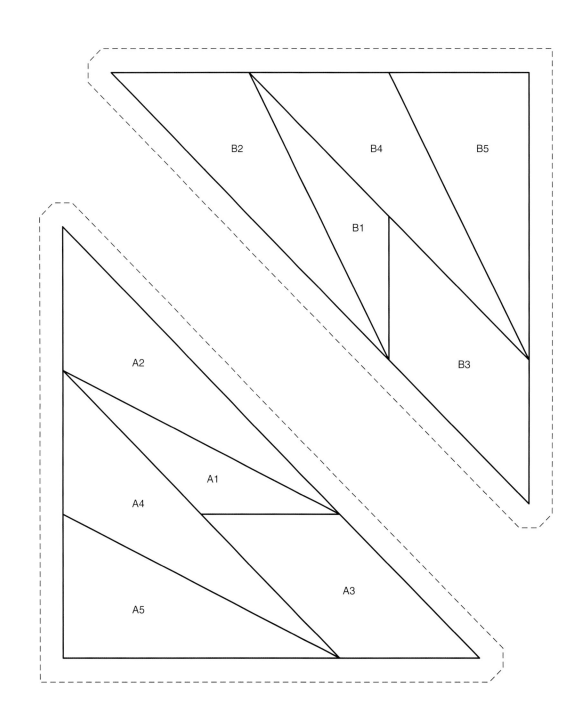

**Amish-Inspired
Quilts**
for Today's Home

Quilt Top Assembly

1. Lay out your quilt in straight set rows as shown in the layout guide.

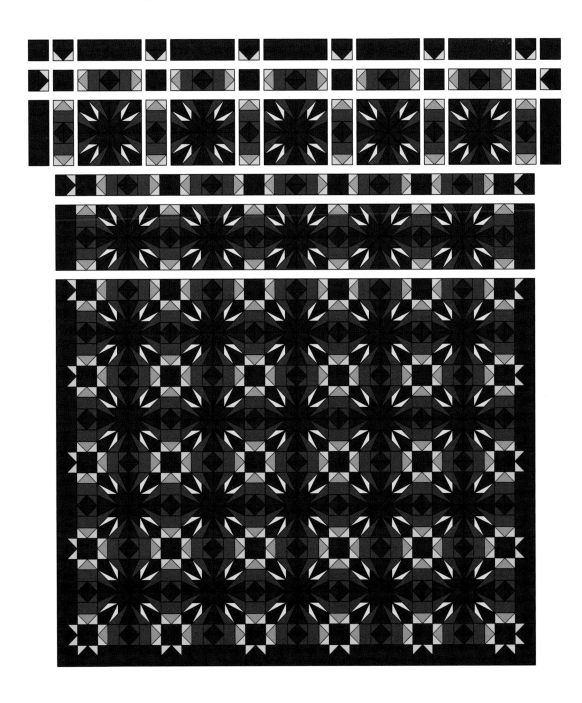

2. Create the borders by sewing the mini flying geese units to the 3 1/2" x 9 1/2" rectangles. The number of mini flying geese units and rectangles will depend on the number of blocks in your quilt.

3. Sew the side borders first, matching the mini flying geese units to the ends of the flying geese sashing units.

4. Sew a Y square to each end of the remaining border pieces and attach to the top and bottom of the quilt.

By Carl Hentsch

Crib

Twin

Layout Guide for All Sizes

Amish-Inspired
Quilts
for Today's Home

King Size Quilt

By Carl Hentsch

Amish-Inspired
Quilts
for Today's Home

In Full Bloom

This is a cheery quilt, despite the black background, that goes together quickly with oversized blocks. The blocks also remind me of dragonflies in the air. Inspired by the spring garden, we were fortunate enough to find a spot with cascading flowers for the photos. The quilt fits right in with the hot pink petunias.

Yardage and Cutting Chart

Finished Size	Crib 36" x 54"	Lap 54" x 78"	Double 76" x 90"	Queen 90" x 108"	King 108" x 108"
Black	1 7/8 yards	2 3/4 yards	4 1/3 yards	6 yards	7 yards
Blocks	(1) 7 1/4" strip cut into (4) 7 1/4" B squares	(3) 7 1/4" strips cut into (12) 7 1/4" B squares	(4) 7 1/4" strips cut into (18) 7 1/4" B squares	(5) 7 1/4" strips cut into (24) 7 1/4" B squares	(7) 7 1/4" strips cut into (32) 7 1/4" B squares
	(3) 3 1/2" strips cut into (8) 3 1/2" G squares (8) 3 1/2" x 6 1/2" I rectangles	(7) 3 1/2" strips cut into (24) 3 1/2" G squares (24) 3 1/2" x 6 1/2" I rectangles	(10) 3 1/2" strips cut into (36) 3 1/2" G squares (36) 3 1/2" x 6 1/2" I rectangles	(13) 3 1/2" strips cut into (48) 3 1/2" G squares (48) 3 1/2" x 6 1/2" I rectangles	(17) 3 1/2" strips cut into (64) 3 1/2" G squares (64) 3 1/2" x 6 1/2" I rectangles
	(2) 4 3/4" strips cut into (10) 4 3/4" E squares	(4) 4 3/4" strips cut into (30) 4 3/4" E squares	(6) 4 3/4" strips cut into (45) 4 3/4" E squares	(8) 4 3/4" strips cut into (60) 4 3/4" E squares	(10) 4 3/4" strips cut into (80) 4 3/4" E squares
	(1) 5 1/2" strips cut into (2) 5 1/2" D squares	(1) 5 1/2" strips cut into (6) 5 1/2" D squares	(2) 5 1/2" strips cut into (9) 5 1/2" D squares	(2) 5 1/2" strips cut into (12) 5 1/2" D squares	(3) 5 1/2" strips cut into (16) 5 1/2" D squares
Side Borders	(3) 6 1/2" strips		(4) 2 1/2" strips	(5) 9 1/2" strips	(11) 6 1/2" strips
Top & Bottom Borders	(3) 3 1/2" strips	(7) 3 1/2" strips for **all** borders	(4) 9 1/2" strips	(5) 6 1/2" strips	
Hot Pink	3/8 yard	1 yard	1 1/4 yards	1 5/8 yards	2 yards
Blocks	(1) 4 3/4" strip cut into (8) 4 3/4" E squares	(3) 4 3/4" strips cut into (24) 4 3/4" E squares	(5) 4 3/4" strips cut into (36) 4 3/4" E squares	(6) 4 3/4" strips cut into (48) 4 3/4" E squares	(8) 4 3/4" strips cut into (64) 4 3/4" E squares
	(1) 4 1/4" strip cut into (4) 4 1/4" squares; cut each square on the diagonal twice to yield (16) H triangles	(2) 4 1/4" strips cut into (14) 4 1/4" squares; cut each square on the diagonal twice to yield (56) H triangles	(2) 4 1/4" strips cut into (18) 4 1/4" squares; cut each square on the diagonal twice to yield (72) H triangles	(3) 4 1/4" strips cut into (24) 4 1/4" squares; cut each square on the diagonal twice to yield (96) H	(4) 4 1/4" strips cut into (32) 4 1/4" squares; cut each square on the diagonal twice to yield (128) H triangles

By Carl Hentsch

				triangles	
	(1) 3" strip cut into (8) 3" C squares	(2) 3" strips cut into (24) 3" C squares	(3) 3" strips cut into (36) 3" C squares	(4) 3" strips cut into (48) 3" C squares	(5) 3" strips cut into (64) 3" C squares
Chartreuse	1/8 yard	1/3 yard	1/2 yard	5/8 yard	7/8 yard
Blocks	(1) 3 7/8" strip cut into (8) 3 7/8" A squares	(3) 3 7/8" strips cut into (24) 3 7/8"A squares	(4) 3 7/8" strips cut into (36) 3 7/8" A squares	(5) 3 7/8" strips cut into (48) 3 7/8" A squares	(7) 3 7/8" strips cut into (64) 3 7/8" A squares
Blue	1/8 yard	1/3 yard	1/2 yard	5/8 yard	7/8 yard
Blocks	(1) 3 7/8" strip cut into (8) 3 7/8" A squares	(3) 3 7/8" strips cut into (24) 3 7/8"A squares	(4) 3 7/8" strips cut into (36) 3 7/8" A squares	(5) 3 7/8" strips cut into (48) 3 7/8"A squares	(7) 3 7/8" strips cut into (64) 3 7/8" A squares
Orange	1/4 yard	2/3 yard	7/8 yard	1 1/8 yards	1 1/2 yards
Blocks	(1) 7 1/4" strip cut into (4) 7 1/4" squares; cut each square on the diagonal twice to yield (16) F triangles	(3) 7 1/4" strips cut into (12) 7 1/4" squares; cut each square on the diagonal twice to yield (48) F triangles	(4) 7 1/4" strips cut into (18) 7 1/4" squares; cut each square on the diagonal twice to yield (72) F triangles	(5) 7 1/4" strips cut into (24) 7 1/4" squares; cut each square on the diagonal twice to yield (96) F triangles	(7) 7 1/4" strips cut into (32) 7 1/4" squares; cut each square on the diagonal twice to yield (128) F triangles
Purple	1/2 yard	7/8 yard	1 yard	1 1/4 yard	1 ! yard
Blocks	(1) 3 1/2" strip cut into (8) 3 1/2" G squares	(3) 3 1/2" strip cut into (24) 3 1/2" G squares	(4) 3 1/2" strip cut into (36) 3 1/2" G squares	(5) 3 1/2" strip cut into (48) 3 1/2" G squares	(6) 3 1/2" strip cut into (64) 3 1/2" G squares
Binding	(5) 2 1/4" strips	(7) 2 1/4" strips	(9) 2 1/4" strips	(11) 2 1/4" strips	(12) 2 1/4" strips
Backing	2 5/8 yards	5 yards	8 1/4 yards	8 2/3 yards	10 yards

	Crib	Lap	Double	Queen	King
Number of blocks needed	2	6	9	12	16

Follow the General Piecing instructions on page 6 to assemble the flying geese.

Large Flying Geese

Make 4 for each block.

To make four large flying geese use

(1) Black B square, (2) Chartreuse A squares and (2) Blue A squares.

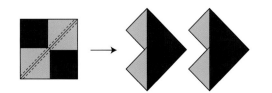
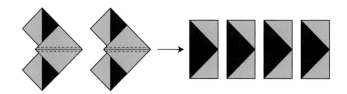

42

Small Flying Geese

Make 4 for each block.

To make four small flying geese units use **(1)** Black D square and **(4)** Hot Pink C squares.

Block Assembly

1. Sew **(2)** Hot Pink H triangles to a G Purple square. Make four for each block.

2. Sew a Hot Pink E square and a small flying geese unit to the unit created in step 1.

3. Sew **(2)** units created in Step 2 to opposite sides of a Black E square.

4. Sew **(2)** Orange F triangles to a Black E square. Make four for each block.

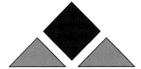 

5. Sew **(2)** triangles created in the previous step to a unit from Step 2. Make two for each block.

6. Lay out your sections and sew together as shown.

7. Sew a large flying geese unit to each side of a Black I rectangle. Make four for each block.

8. Sew a Black G square to each side of two of the units.

9. Sew the two short units to each side of your block. Then complete the block by attaching the longer units to the top and bottom.

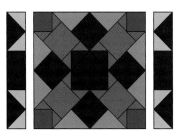

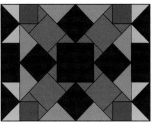

10. Make the number of blocks required for your selected size.

By Carl Hentsch

Quilt Top Assembly

1. Sew the blocks into rows and then sew the rows together.
For example, for the lap size you will need three rows of two blocks each.

2. Measure your quilt from top to bottom. Cut the side borders strips to length and attach to your quilt.

3. Now measure your quilt from side to side. Once again, cut the borders strips to length and attach to your quilt. Note that the top and bottom borders are not always the same width as the side borders.

Amish-Inspired
Quilts
for Today's Home

Crib　　　　Lap　　　Queen/Double　　　　King

Double

Queen

Layout Guide for All Sizes

By Carl Hentsch

45

Amish-Inspired
Quilts
for Today's Home

Finished Quilt

By Carl Hentsch

Sunday Picnic

This is another large block quilt that goes together quickly. The quilt is reminiscent of children running in the park with pinwheels held high in the air, on a Sunday afternoon after church.

Finished Size	Crib 42" x 59"	Lap 59" x 76"	Twin 59" x 93"	Queen 93" x 110"	King 110" x 110"
Black Print	1 3/4 yards	2 3/4 yards	3 1/4 yards	5 3/4 yards	6 3/4 yards
Blocks	(3) 7 1/4" strips. Cut each strip into (12) 7 1/4" E squares	(5) 7 1/4" strips. Cut each strip into (24) 7 1/4" E squares	(6) 7 1/4" strips. Cut each strip into (30) 7 1/4" E squares	(12) 7 1/4" strips. Cut each strip in (60) 7 1/4" E squares	(15) 7 1/4" strips. Cut each strip into (72) 7 1/4" E squares
	(2) 9 3/4" strips. Cut each strip into (6) 9 3/4" squares. Cut each square on the diagonal twice to yield (24) F triangles	(3) 9 3/4" strips. Cut each strip into (12) 9 3/4" squares. Cut each square on the diagonal twice to yield (48) F triangles	(4) 9 3/4" strips. Cut each strip into (15) 9 3/4" squares. Cut each square on the diagonal twice to yield (60) F triangles	(8) 9 3/4" strips. Cut each strip into (30) 9 3/4" squares. Cut each square on the diagonal twice to yield (120) F triangles	(9) 9 3/4" strips. Cut each strip into (36) 9 3/4" squares. Cut each square on the diagonal twice to yield (144) F triangles
Outer Border	(5) 3 1/2" strips	(7) 3 1/2" strips	(8) 3 1/2" strips	(11) 3 1/2" strips	(12) 3 1/2" strips
Black Solid	2/3 yard	7/8 yards	1 yard	1 1/4 yards	1 1/3 yards
Inner Border	(5) 1 1/2" strips	(7) 1 1/2" strips	(8) 1 1/2" strips	(10) 1 1/2" strips	(11) 1 1/2" strips
Binding	(6) 2 1/4" strips	(7) 2 1/4" strips	(9) 2 1/4" strips	(11) 2 1/4" strips	(12) 2 1/4" strips
Purple	3/8 yard	5/8 yard	2/3 yard	1 1/3 yards	1 3/4 yards
	(3) 3 7/8" strips. Cut each strip into (24) 3 7/8" D squares	(5) 3 7/8" strips. Cut each strip into (48) 3 7/8" D squares	(6) 3 7/8" strips. Cut each strip into (60) 3 7/8" D squares	(12) 3 7/8" strips. Cut each strip into (120) 3 7/8" D squares	(15) 3 7/8" strips. Cut each strip into (144) 3 7/8" D squares
Violet	3/8 yard	5/8 yard	2/3 yard	1 1/3 yards	1 3/4 yards
	(3) 3 7/8" strips. Cut each strip into (24) 3 7/8" D squares	(5) 3 7/8" strips. Cut each strip into (48) 3 7/8" D squares	(6) 3 7/8" strips. Cut each strip into (60) 3 7/8" D squares	(12) 3 7/8" strips. Cut each strip into (120) 3 7/8" D squares	(15) 3 7/8" strips. Cut each strip into (144) 3 7/8" D squares
Blue	1/2 yard	1 yard	1 1/4 yards	2 1/4 yards	2 3/4 yards
	(2) 5 1/2" strips. Cut each strip into (12) 5 1/2" squares. Cut each square on the diagonal	(4) 5 1/2" strips. Cut each strip into (24) 5 1/2" squares. Cut each square on the diagonal	(5) 5 1/2" strips. Cut each strip into (30) 5 1/2" squares. Cut each square on the diagonal	(9) 5 1/2" strips. Cut each strip into (60) 5 1/2" squares. Cut each square on the diagonal	(11) 5 1/2" strips. Cut each strip into (72) 5 1/2" squares. Cut each square on the diagonal

By Carl Hentsch

49

	twice to yield (48) C triangles	twice to yield (96) C triangles	twice to yield (120) C triangles	twice to yield (240) C triangles	twice to yield (288) C triangles
	(2) 3" strips. Cut each strip into (24) 3" squares. Cut each square on the diagonal once to yield (48) B triangles	(4) 3" strips. Cut each strip into (48) 3" squares. Cut each square on the diagonal once to yield (96) B triangles	(5) 3" strips Cut each strip into (60) 3" squares. Cut each square on the diagonal once to yield (120) B triangles	(10) 3" strips. Cut each strip into (120) 3" squares. Cut each square on the diagonal once to yield (240) B triangles	(12) 3" strips. Cut each strip into (144) 3" squares. Cut each square on the diagonal once to yield (288) B triangles
Orange	1/8 yard	1/4 yard	3/8 yard	1/2 yard	5/8 yard
	(1) 3" strip. Cut each strip into (12) 3" squares. Cut each square on the diagonal once to yield (24) B triangles	(2) 3" strips. Cut each strip into (24) 3" squares. Cut each square on the diagonal once to yield (48) B triangles	(3) 3" strips. Cut each strip into (30) 3" squares. Cut each square on the diagonal once to yield (60) B triangles	(5) 3" strips. Cut each strip into (60) 3" squares. Cut each square on the diagonal once to yield (120) B triangles	(6) 3" strips. Cut each strip into (72) 3" squares. Cut each square on the diagonal once to yield (144) B triangles
Green	1/8 yard	1/4 yard	3/8 yard	1/2 yard	5/8 yard
	(1) 3" strip cut into (12) 3" squares. Cut each square on the diagonal once to yield (24) B triangles	(2) 3" strips cut into (24) 3" squares. Cut each square on the diagonal once to yield (48) B triangles	(3) 3" strips cut into (30) 3" squares. Cut each square on the diagonal once to yield (60) B triangles	(5) 3" strips cut into (60) 3" squares. Cut each square on the diagonal once to yield (120) B triangles	(6) 3" strips cut into (72) 3" squares. Cut each square on the diagonal once to yield (144) B triangles
Backing	2 7/8 yards	4 5/8 yards	5 5/8 yards	8 1/2 yards	10 yards

See page 51 (For each block you will need)

	Crib	Lap	Twin	Queen	King
Blocks	6	12	15	30	36

Amish-Inspired
Quilts
for Today's Home

Sunday Picnic Block
17" square finished

Block Assembly

1. Take **(8)** Blue B triangles, **(4)** Green B triangles and **(4)** Orange B triangles. Sew them in pairs as shown.

For each block you will need
(4) Blue/Green pairs and **(4)** Blue/Orange pairs.

2. Sew a C triangle to the bottom of each Blue/Green pair.

3. Sew a C triangle to the side of the Blue/Orange pairs.

4. Sew your (4) Blue/Green squares together to make the block center.

5. Following the General Instructions on page 6, make the flying geese units.

For each block you will need

(2) Black E squares. Use **(4)** Purple D squares with one black print E square and **(4)** Violet D squares with the other black print E square.

6. Sew a purple and violet flying geese unit into a square. Make four for each block.

7. Adding **(4)** F triangles per block, assemble into diagonal rows and then sew the rows together to complete the block.

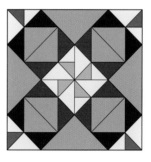

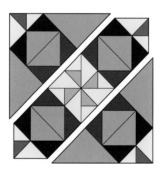

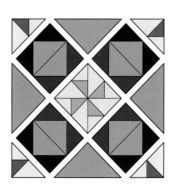

By Carl Hentsch

51

Quilt Top Assembly

1. Lay out the required number of blocks. Sew the blocks together into rows, and then sew the rows together to complete the top. For example, you will need four rows of three blocks each for a twin-size quilt.

2. Measure your quilt from top to bottom. Cut the side borders to length and attach to your quilt.

3. Measure your quilt from side to side. Cut the top and bottom borders to length and attach to your quilt.

4. Quilt and bind.

Layout Guide for All Sizes

By Carl Hentsch

Amish-Inspired
Quilts
for Today's Home

Crib Size Quilt

By Carl Hentsch

House on the Prairie

Amish-Inspired
Quilts
for Today's Home

Finished Quilt Size: 72" x 84"
Finished block size: 8 1/2" square

I wanted to create a different house block than is typically seen. I turned this block on point, but it can also be used in straight sets. I kept my original color theme for the houses but varied them with lights, mediums and darks. I also used a background fabric that reminded me of the night sky. Just imagine how dark and lonely it would have been – a solitary house out in the prairie with only candles to light the evening

Fabric Requirements
3 fat quarters each of 5 different fabrics (choose a Light, Medium and Dark for each color).
I used Green, Purple, Pink, Yellow and Blue Black Print:
4 2/3 yards for background Backing: 5 1/8 yards Binding: 2/3 yard

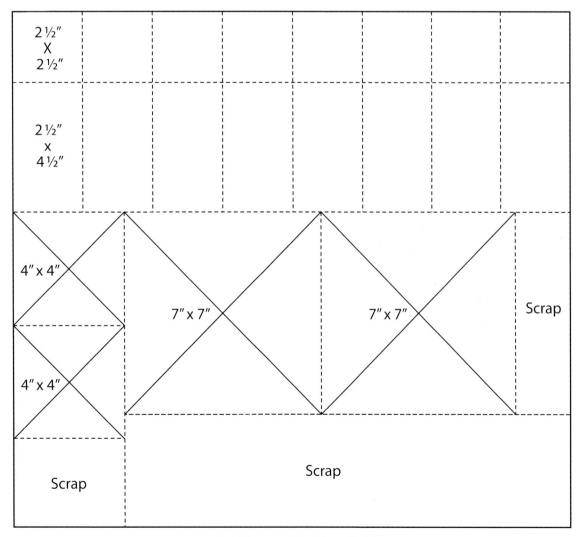

Fat Quarter Cutting Guide

By Carl Hentsch

Cutting

1. Follow the Cutting Guide to cut your fat quarters. You will be able to cut four blocks from each fat quarter.

2. Draw a diagonal line on the wrong side of each 2 1/2" square.

3. From the background fabric, cut:

(6) 7" strips cut into (30) 7" squares. Cut each square on the diagonal twice to yield (120) large triangles.

(8) 4 1/2" strips. Cut these strips into (120) 2 1/2" x 4 1/2" rectangles.

(3) 4" strips cut into (30) 4" squares. Cut each square on the diagonal twice to yield (120) small triangles.

(8) 2 1/2" strips cut into (120) 2 1/2" squares.

Draw a diagonal line on the wrong side of each square but do not cut. **(8)** 6 1/2" border strips

Block Assembly
The following instructions are for one block.
Make 50 blocks.

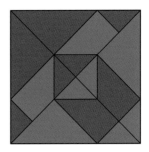

From each fat quarter:
(2) 2 1/2" squares
(2) 2 1/2" x 4 1/2" rectangles
(2) Large triangles
(2) Small triangles

From the background fabric:
(2) 2 1/2" squares
(2) 2 1/2" x 4 1/2" rectangles
(2) large triangles

1. Place a color 2 1/2" square on a background 2 1/2" x 4" rectangle, right sides together.

2. Sew on the line drawn on the square.

3. Trim 1/4" from the sewn line. Press open.

4. Repeat Steps 1 – 3 with a background square and a color rectangle.

Amish-Inspired
Quilts
for Today's Home

5. Assemble the block as shown. Make 50 blocks.

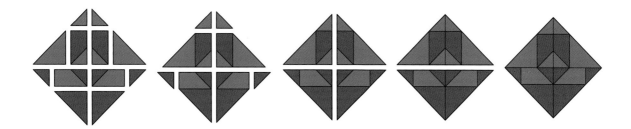

Setting Triangle Assembly
The setting triangles are made from partially finished blocks.

From the remaining fabric pieces, make (4) corner triangles, (10) side setting triangles and (8) top and bottom setting triangles.

1. Make (1) block but only sew the quarters, as shown. Do not sew the quarters to each other. Make four quarter blocks.

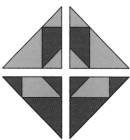

2. Make (5) blocks but only sew the vertical halves together. Make ten side setting triangles.

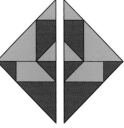

3. Make (4) blocks but only sew the horizontal halves together to make (4) half-blocks for a total of (8) top and bottom setting triangles

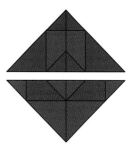

By Carl Hentsch

Quilt Top Assembly

1. Lay out your quilt as shown in diagonal rows.

2. Measure your quilt from top to bottom. Cut the 6 1/2" border strips to this length and attach to the sides of your quilt.

3. Measure your quilt from side to side. Once again, cut the border strips to this length and attach to the top and bottom of your quilt.

4. Quilt as desired and bind.

Amish-Inspired
Quilts
for Today's Home

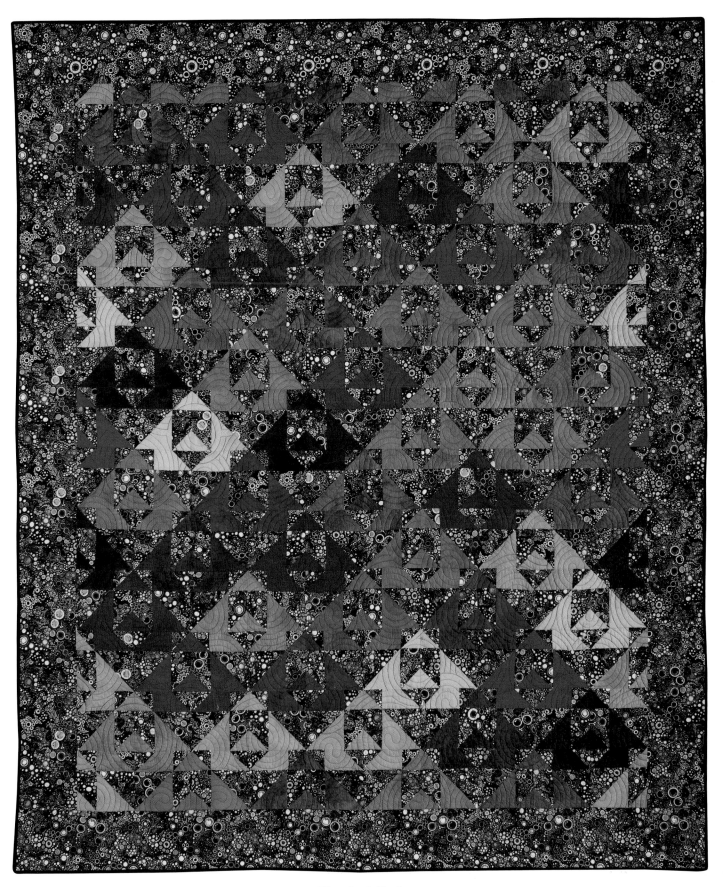

Finished Quilt

By Carl Hentsch

A Formal Affair

Finished size: 72" x 81"

While Sunday Picnic is for the children, this quilt was inspired by a formal gathering of adults, maybe a wedding or other special event. I have always been fond of large star quilts, and I made this one slightly different by designing the star with only six points. The large diamonds were also a great opportunity for me to fussy cut some fabric for the center and outer points of the star. I decided on a background of periwinkle to represent a gathering twilight with hanging lanterns illuminating the space.

Amish-Inspired
Quilts
for Today's Home

	Periwinkle Solid	2 1/3 yards
		(2) 18 3/4" x 33" strips (2) 18 1/2" x width of fabric (WOF) strips (2) 11 1/4" x 19 1/4" rectangles
A	Large Scale Print	2/3 yard
		(3) 6 1/2" strips cut into (12) 60-degree diamonds
	Note: If you are going to fussy cut your fabric, cut (6) identical diamonds for the star center and (6) for the star points. Depending on the size of the pattern repeat, you will need between 2 and 2 1/2 yards of this print for fussy cutting.	
B	Light Blue Pint	1 1/4 yard
		(3) 6 1/2" strips cut into (12) 60-degree diamonds
		(4) 5" strips cut into (13) 5" x 9 1/2" rectangles
C	Dark Blue Print	1 1/3 yards
		(5) 6 1/2" strips cut into (18) 60-degree diamonds
		(2) 5" strips cut into (6) 5" x 9 1/2" rectangles
D	Medium Pink/Blue Print	1 1/4 yard
		(3) 6 1/2" strips cut into (12) 60-degree diamonds
		(4) 5" strips cut into (14) 5" x 9 1/2" rectangles
	Navy Blue	5/8 yard
		(8) 2 1/4" strips for binding
	Backing	4 yards

Additional Supplies

Template plastic (if you plan on fussy cutting the star centers and points)
Quilting ruler with a 60-degree mark

Cutting 60-Degree Diamonds

1. Align the ruler's 60-degree line with the edge of the strip.
Using a rotary cutter, trim off the end of the fabric.

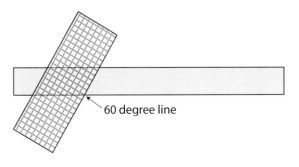

60 degree line

By Carl Hentsch

63

2. With the 60-degree line still on the edge of the strip, find the 6 1/2" line on your ruler. Match that line with the angled left edge of the fabric.

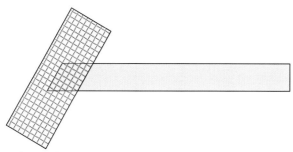

3 . Cut along the ruler for your first shape. Continue cutting the number of diamond segments specified for each of the four fabrics.

Fussy Cutting (Optional)

Using the 60-degree diamond template on page 67:

1. Trace the template onto the template plastic and cut it out on the traced line using a pair of sharp utility scissors.

Note: The template includes a 1/4" seam allowance.

2. To determine the section on your fabric that you want to fussy cut, position the template plastic over some of the key features, checking to see how the pattern fits the template.

3. When you have chosen the areas to fussy cut, trace around the template with a pencil or permanent marker. Remove the template and carefully cut out the diamond with your scissors or a rotary cutter and ruler. Be careful not to cut too far away from the marking because you don't want to cut into another section that you might use.

4. Reposition the plastic template on the next section, trace and cut. Continue in this manner until you have cut all the required pieces.

Assemble the Large Diamond Units

1. Each large diamond is made from (12) small 60-degree diamonds. You will make (3) different strips using these small diamonds. Refer to he illustration for the fabric placement in each strip. Make (6) of each strip.

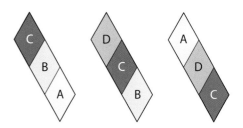

2. Sew the rows together to make the large diamonds.

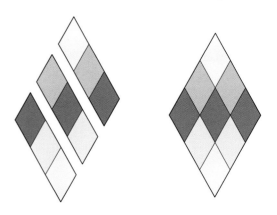

Background Pieces

1. Place the (2) 18 3/4" x WOF strips wrong sides together. Align the 60-degree line on your ruler with the long edge of the strip. Using a rotary cutter, trim off the end of the fabric.

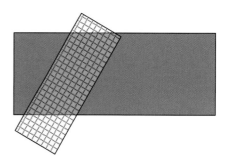

2. Measure 21 7/8" along the bottom of the strip and place a mark. Align your ruler with the lower angled edge on the mark and with the upper edge at the edge of the fabric, as shown. Cut along the ruler to make a large 60-degree triangle.

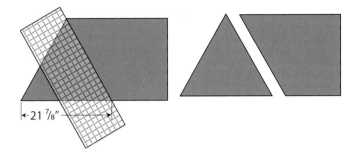

3. Measure 21 7/8" along the top of the strip and place a mark. Line your ruler with the mark and the lower left angle and cut along the ruler to make another large 60-degree triangle. You should now have four large triangles.

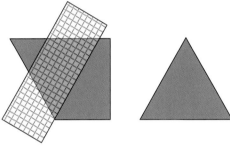

4. Place the (2) 18 1/2" x 32 1/4" strips wrong sides together. Measure 21 1/2" from the upper left corner and place a mark. Now measure 21 1/2" from the lower right corner and place a mark. Align your ruler between these marks and cut to make the pieces. You should have (2) right angle pieces and (2) left angle pieces.

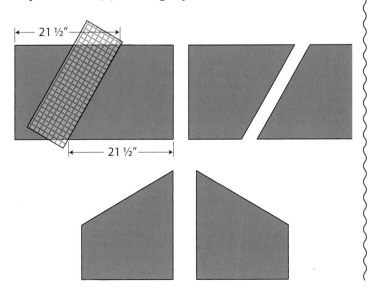

5. Place the (2) 11" x 19 1/4" rectangles wrong sides together. Cut in half diagonally to yield (4) triangles.

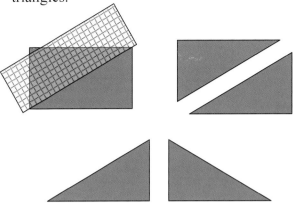

Quilt Top Assembly

1. Sew two large 60-degree triangles to a large 60-degree diamond as shown. Note: Make sure the two light small diamonds are at the bottom of the large diamond. Make two.

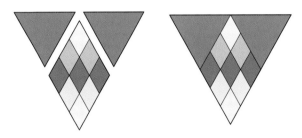

2. Sew the remaining background pieces to the large diamonds as shown. Make two.

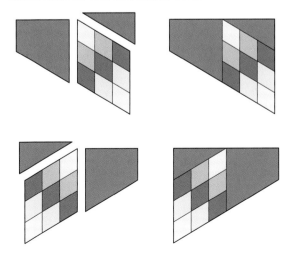

3. Arrange the sections as illustrated and sew together to complete the top.

4. Sew (8) 5 ½" x 9 ½" rectangles together to make a border strip. Make four.

5. Attach the side borders first, then attach the top and bottom borders.

Amish-Inspired
Quilts
for Today's Home

FA Diamond Template

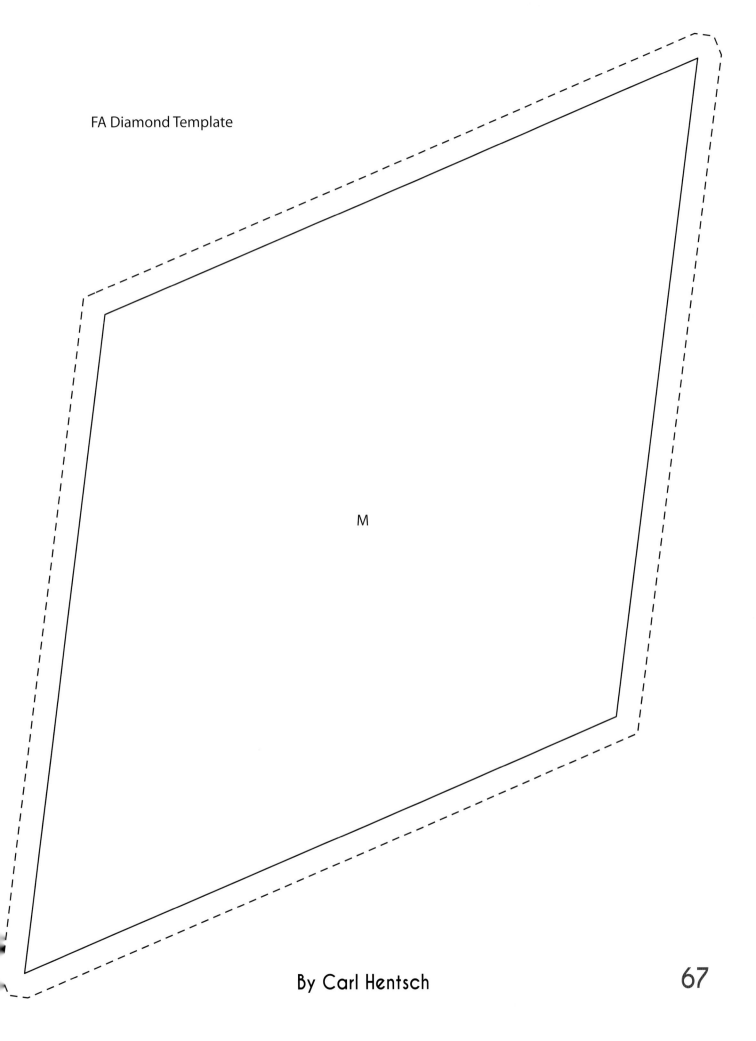

M

By Carl Hentsch

68

Finished Quilt

By Carl Hentsch

Amish-Inspired
Quilts
for Today's Home

A New Barn Raising

Finished size: 72"x 72"

Who doesn't love a log cabin quilt? I wanted to take this quilt a step further and incorporate the log cabin block into a star setting. Think of this as a lone star quilt made with log cabins and not the typical 45-degree diamonds that you usually see. Take your time, and you will end up with an amazing quilt.

Yardage and Cutting Chart

Cut the strip(s) indicated in Column 2; from these strips cut the squares or rectangles indicated in Column 3.

Yardage and Cutting Chart

Cut the strip(s) indicated in Column 1 by the width of the fabric. From these strips cut the squares or rectangles indicated in Column 2.

First Cut	Second Cut
Block 1 (Diamond A)	
Deep Violet: 1/8 yard	
(1) 2 1/4" strip	(8) 2 1/4" 45-degree R diamonds
Dark Violet: 1/4 yard	
(4) 1 3/8" strips	(8) 6" T rectangles (8) 7 1/2" U rectangles
Medium Violet: 1/4 yard	
(4) 1 3/8" strips	(8) 8 1/2" V rectangles (8) 9 1/2" W rectangles
Light Violet: 1/3 yard	
(6) 1 3/8" strips	(8) 11" X rectangles (8) 12" Y rectangles
Block 2 (Log Cabin Square)	
Deep Purple: 1/8 yard	
(1) 3" strip	(8) 3" A squares
Dark Purple: 1/8 yard	
(2) 1 3/4" strips	(8) 4 1/4" C rectangles (8) 5 1/2" D rectangles
Medium Purple: 1/4 yard	
(4) 1 3/4" strips	(8) 6 3/4" E rectangles (8) 8" F rectangles
Light Purple: 1/3 yard	
(5) 1 1/4" strips	(8) 10 1/2" H rectangles (8) 9 1/4" G rectangles
Block 3 (Diamond Block B)	
Deep Blue: 1/4 yard	
(2) 2 1/4" strips	(24) 2 1/4" 45-degree R diamonds
Dark Blue: 1/2yard	
(9) 1 3/8" strips	(24) 7 1/2" U rectangles (24) 6" T rectangles
Medium Blue: 1/2 yard	

By Carl Hentsch

71

| (12) 1 3/8" strips | (24) 8 1/2" V rectangles |
| | (24) 9 1/2" W rectangles |

| (16) 1 3/8" strips | (24) 12" Y rectangles |
| | (24) 11" X rectangles |

Block 4 (Log Cabin Square and Log Cabin Setting Triangles)

Deep Green: 1/4 yard

(1) 3 3/8" strip	(4) 3 3/8" squares. Cut each square on the diagonal
(1) 3" strip	once to yield (8) J triangles.
	(12) 3" A squares

Dark Green: 1/2 yard

(7) 1 3/4" strips	(8) 5" K rectangles,
	(8) 6 1/2" L rectangles,
	(12) 4 1/4" C rectangles
	(12) 5 1/2" D rectangles

Medium Green: 5/8 yard

(10) 1 3/4" strips	(8) 7 1/2" M rectangles
	(8) 9" N rectangles
	(12) 6 3/4" E rectangles
	(12) 8" F rectangles

Light Green: 2/3 yard

(12) 1 3/4" strips	(8) 10" P rectangles
	(8) 11 1/2" Q rectangles
	(12) 9 1/4" G rectangles
	(12) 10 1/2" H rectangles

All blocks

Gray Chevron: 3 5/8 yards

(44) 1 3/8" strips	(32) 4 1/2" S rectangles
	(32) 6" T rectangles
	(32) 7 1/2" U rectangles
	(32) 8 1/2" V rectangles
	(32) 9 1/2" W rectangles
	(32) 11" X rectangles
(21) 1 3/4" strips	(20) 9 1/4" G rectangles
	(20) 8" F rectangles
	(20) 6 3/4" E rectangles
	(20) 5 1/2" D rectangles
	(20) 4 1/4" C rectangles
	(20) 3" B rectangles
(8) 2 1/2" border strips	

Binding

Deep Purple or Black: 5/8 yard

(7) 2 1/4" strips

Assemble Log Cabin Blocks 1 & 2

1. Lay out your pieces as shown in the diagram. The letters represent the piece you cut, and the number indicates the sewing order.

2. Place the B rectangle and A square right sides together and sew along the long edge. Press toward B.

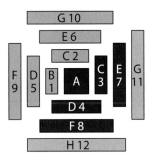

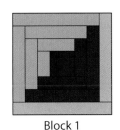

Block 1
Make 8

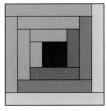

Block 2
Make 8

3. Continue adding rectangles clockwise around the A square, always pressing toward the piece just added.

Assemble the Log Cabin Setting Triangles

1. Lay out the pieces for the setting triangles as shown. Following the same method as above, sew each piece to the J triangle in a clockwise fashion.

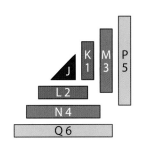

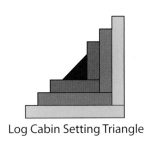

Log Cabin Setting Triangle

2. The rectangles will be longer than the center triangle. Take your ruler and place the 45-degree line on the long edge of the block, as shown, aligning the edge of the ruler with the center triangle.

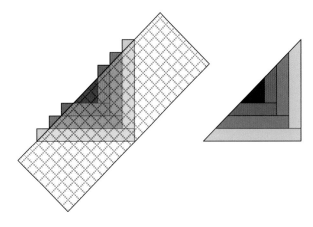

3. Cut off the extra to make your setting triangles. Make eight.

Assemble the Log Cabin Diamond Block A

1. Lay out your pieces for Diamond Block A as shown. Like the triangle units, each piece is cut larger and will be trimmed to size after it is sewn together.

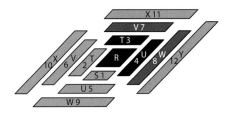

2. Beginning at the center and continuing clockwise around the diamond, sew and trim each piece in the order indicated by the number on the piece.

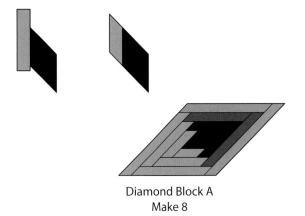

Diamond Block A
Make 8

By Carl Hentsch

Assemble the Log Cabin Diamond Block B

1. Lay out your pieces for Diamond Block B exactly as you did for Diamond Block A and assemble the blocks in the same manner.

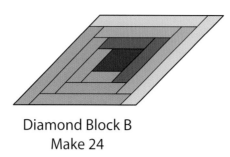

Diamond Block B
Make 24

Quilt Top Assembly

Follow the general piecing instructions for Y seams on page 7
.

1. Sew the A Diamonds together into pairs using partial seams. Make sure the Fabric 1 diamonds meet in the center.

2. Using (1) Log Cabin Block and (2) Log Cabin B Diamonds, assemble four side units as shown.

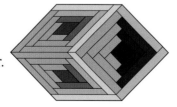

3. Attach the four side units to the center.

Amish-Inspired
Quilts
for Today's Home

4. Using the remaining Log Cabin Blocks and B Diamonds to assemble four corner units.

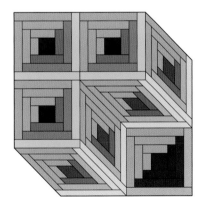

5. Lay out the center section and the (4) corner units and assemble with the (4) triangles. This diagram may help you put the various units together.

6. Measure your quilt from top to bottom. Cut the side borders to length and attach to your quilt

7. Measure your quilt from side to side. Cut the top and bottom borders to length and attach to your quilt.

8. Quilt and bind.

Amish-Inspired
Quilts
for Today's Home

Finished Quilt

By Carl Hentsch

Sun Catcher

Finished Size: 64" x 64"

This quilt is another variation on the lone star quilt and also uses a variation on the log cabin block. When I look at this quilt, I am reminded of glass ornaments hanging in the window, radiating prisms of colored light around the room.

Note: For each block, it is critical that you follow the instructions exactly or the color patterns will not be correct.

Amish-Inspired
Quilts
for Today's Home

#	Color	Yardage	Cutting
1	Yellow	1/4 yard	(1) 1 5/8" A1 strip. (2) 1 1/4" A2 strips
2	Garnet	1/4 yard	(1) 1 5/8" A1 strip. (2) 1 1/4" A2 strips
3	Amber	1/4 yard	(1) 1 5/8" strip cut into (8) 2 3/4" x 1 5/8" B1 rectangles (3) 1 1/4" strip cut into (24) 4 1/2" x 1 1/4" B2 rectangles
4	Crimson	1/4 yard	(1) 1 5/8" strip cut into (8) 2 3/4" x 1 5/8" B1 rectangles (3) 1 1/4" strips cut into (24) 4 1/2" x 1 1/4" B2 rectangles
5	Orange	1/4 yard	(1) 1 5/8" strip cut into (8) 3 7/8" x 1 5/8" C1 rectangles (4) 1 1/4" strips cut into (24) 5 1/2" x 1 1/4" C2 rectangles
6	Amethyst	1/4 yard	(1) 1 5/8" strip cut into (8) 3 7/8" x 1 5/8" C1 rectangles (4) 1 1/4" strips cut into (24) 5 1/2" x 1 1/4" C2 rectangles
7	Emerald	1/4 yard	(1) 1 5/8" strip cut into (8) 5" x 1 5/8" D1 rectangles (4) 1 1/4" strips cut into (24) 6 1/2" x 1 1/4" D2 rectangles
8	Tangerine	1/4 yard	(1) 1 5/8" strip cut into (8) 5" x 1 5/8" D1 rectangles (4) 1 1/4" strips cut into (24) 6 1/2" x 1 1/4" D2 rectangles
9	Clear Blue	1/3 yard	(2) 1 5/8" strips cut into (8) 6 1/8" x 1 5/8" E1 rectangles (5) 1 1/4" strips cut into (24) 8" x 1 1/4" E2 rectangles
10	Country Red	1/3 yard	(2) 1 5/8" strips cut into (8) 6 1/8" x 1 5/8" E1 rectangles (5) 1 " " strips cut into (24) 8" x 1 1/4" E2 rectangles
11	Turquoise	1/3 yard	(2) 1 5/8" strips cut into (8) 7 1/4" x 1 5/8" F1 rectangles (6) 1 1/4" strips cut into (24) 9" x 1 1/4" F2 rectangles
12	Magenta	1/3 yard	(2) 1 5/8" strips cut into (8) 7 1/4" x 1 5/8" F1 rectangles (6) 1 1/4" strips cut into (24) 9" x 1 1/4" F2 rectangles
13	Blue	1/3 yard	(2) 1 5/8" strips cut into (8) 8 3/8" x 1 5/8" G1 rectangles (6) 1 1/4" strips cut into (24) 10" x 1 1/4" G2 rectangles
14	Reddish Purple	1/3 yard	(2) 1 5/8" strips cut into (8) 8 3/8" x 1 5/8" G1 rectangles (6) 1 1/4" strips cut into (24) 10" x 1 1/4" G2 rectangles
15	Indigo	1/2 yard	(2) 1 5/8" strips cut into (8) 9 1/2" x 1 5/8" H1 rectangles (8) 1 1/4" strips cut into (24) 11 1/2" x 1 1/4" H2 rectangles
16	Gray Solid	2 1/8 yards	(3) 9 1/4" strips cut into (12) 9 1/4" X squares (2) 6 3/4" strips cut into (8) 6 3/4" 45-degree Y diamonds (see page X on how to cut) (1) 13 3/4" strip cut into (2) 13 3/4" squares. Cut each square on the diagonal twice to yield (8) Z quarter square triangles (8) 2 1/2" border strips
17	Black	1/2 yard for binding	(7) 2 1/4" strips

By Carl Hentsch

Log Cabin Block

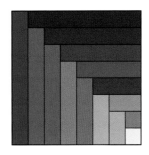

Note: For each block it is critical that you follow the instructions exactly or the color patterns will not be correct.

1. Sew the Fabric #1 and #2 A1 strips together to make a strip set. Cut the strip set into (8) 1 5/8" x 2 3/4" rectangles.

2. With Fabric #1 on the bottom, sew a Fabric #3 B1 strip to the left side.

3. Sew a Fabric 4 B1 strip to the top of the unit created above.

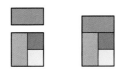

4. Continue in this manner, adding the fabric strips in order. (NOTE: Odd-number fabrics are always on the left on the unit and even numbers on the top.)

  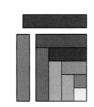  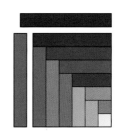

5. Complete the block by adding the Fabric #15 H1 rectangle to the left side. Square up the block to measure 9 1/4".

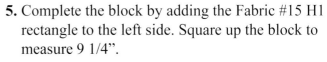
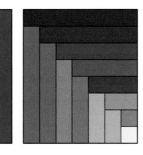 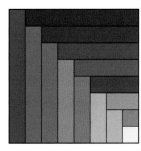

Diamond A Block

Diamond A Block
Finished size 6 ¾"
Make 8

1. Sew a Fabric #1 and #2 A2 strip together into a strip set, offsetting the ends by 1".

Amish-Inspired Quilts
for Today's Home

2. Align the 45-degree line on your ruler along the edge of the fabric or along the seam line. Using a rotary cutter, trim off the left end of the fabric.

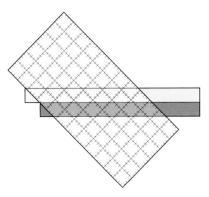

3. Find the 1 1/4" line on your ruler. Match this line with the angled left edge of the fabric and realign the 45-degree line with the fabric edge or seam.

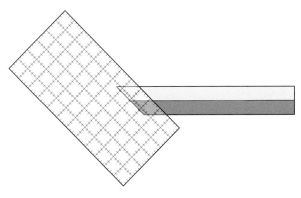

4. Cut along the right side of the ruler to make your first shape. Continue cutting diamond segments until you have (8) 1 1/4" A diamonds.

5. Lay down the A diamond with Fabric #1 at the bottom. Place a Fabric #3 B1 rectangle on top of the diamond, right sides together, with the left edges aligned. Sew in place and press open. Trim the ends of the rectangle even with the diamond.

6. Place a Fabric #4 B1 rectangle on top of the diamond, right sides together, aligned along the top of the unit created in Step 5. Sew in place and press open. Trim the ends even with the diamond.

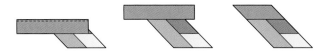

7. Repeat the previous steps, adding the fabrics in numerical order, as you did for the log cabin block.

Diamond B Block

Diamond B Block
Finished size 6 ¾"
Make 16

1. Sew a Fabric #1 and #2 A2 strip together to make a strip set, offsetting the ends by 1".

2. Align the 45-degree line on your ruler with the edge of the fabric or along the seam line. Using a rotary cutter, trim off the end of the fabric.

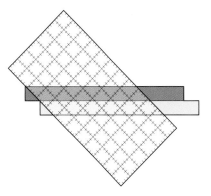

3. Find the 1 1/4" line on your ruler. Match this line with the angled left edge of the fabric and realign the 45-degree line with the fabric edge or the seam.

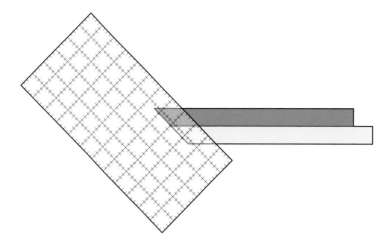

4. Cut along the ruler to make your first shape. Continue cutting diamond segments. Make (16) 1 1/4" B diamonds.

5. Lay the B diamond down with Fabric #1 at the left. Place a Fabric #3 B1 rectangle on top of the diamond, right sides together and aligned with the top edge of the diamond. Sew in place and press open. Trim the ends even with the diamond.

6. Place a Fabric #4 B1 rectangle on top of the unit created in Step 5, right sides together and aligned along the right edge of the diamond, as shown. Sew in place and press open. Trim the ends even with the diamond as above.

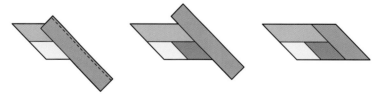

7. Repeat the steps above, adding the fabrics in numerical order as you did for the log cabin blocks.

8. Make (16) 6 3/4" Diamond B blocks.

Amish-Inspired
Quilts
for Today's Home

Quilt Top Assembly

Review the General Instruction for Y seams on page 7.

1. Sew together the A Diamonds into pairs, making sure the Fabric #1 diamonds meet in the center, using partial seams.

2. Assemble four side units using (1) Log Cabin Block and (2) B Diamonds.

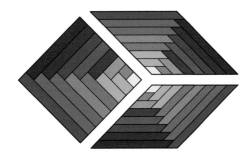

By Carl Hentsch

3. Attach the side units to the center created in Step 1.

**Amish-Inspired
Quilts**
for Today's Home

4. Using the remaining log cabin blocks, B Diamonds and background squares, assemble four corner units.

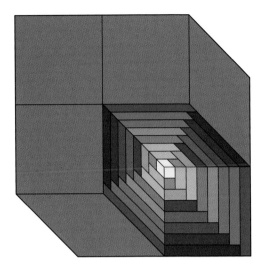

5. Complete the quilt top by sewing the (4) corner units and (4) triangles to the center section as shown in the diagram.

~~~~~~

Finish the Quilt

1. Measure your quilt from side to side. Sew your border strips together and cut to length.
Attach to the top and bottom of your quilt.

2. Now measure your quilt from top to bottom.
Cut your side borders to length and attach to the sides of your quilt.

3. Quilt and bind.

~~~~~~

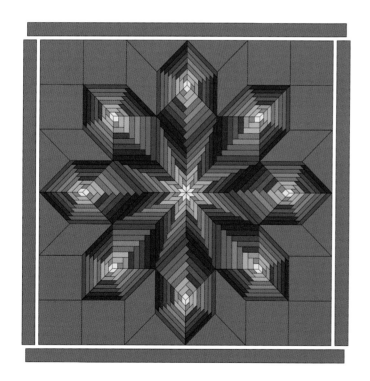

Amish-Inspired
Quilts
for Today's Home

Finished Quilt

By Carl Hentsch

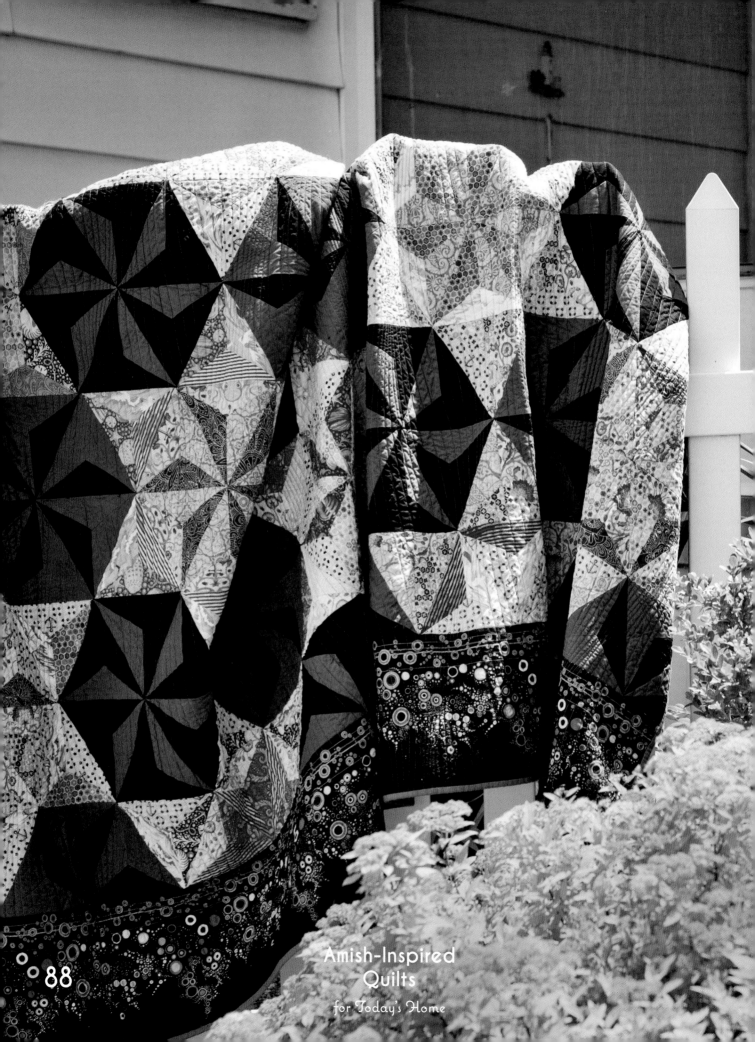

Amish-Inspired
Quilts
for Today's Home

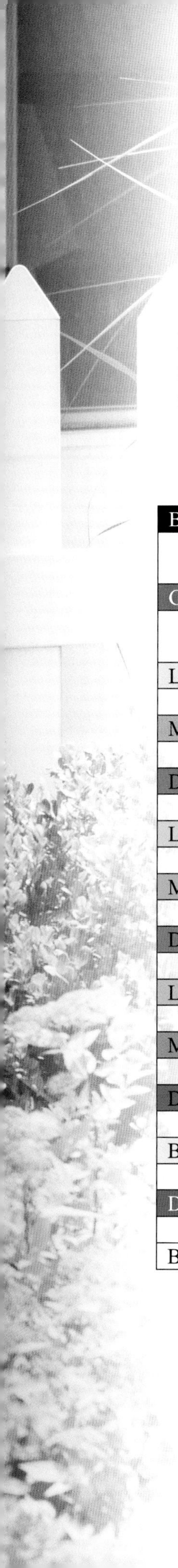

Falling Stars

Finished Size: 93" x 99"

A variation on a hexagon, this quilt is actually quite simple with a specialty ruler. I can just imagine lying on the ground long ago, watching the shooting stars among the vast blanket of the Milky Way.

Yardage and Cutting Chart

Read through all of the instructions before you cut the triangles. In the chart below, triangle refers to a 120-degree triangle, and half triangle refers to a 120-degree triangle cut in half according to the directions.

Black Solid	**3yards**
	(26) 2 1/2" strips cut into (180) triangles
	(14) 2 5/8" strips cut into (90) half triangle pairs
Gray Solid	**3 yards**
	(26) 2 1/2" strips cut into (180) triangles
	(14) 2 5/8" strips cut into (90) half triangle pairs
Light Blue Print	**2/3 yard**
	(8) 2 5/8" strips cut into (60) half triangle pairs
Medium Blue Print	**3/4 yard**
	(9) 2 1/2" strips cut into (60) triangles
Dark Blue Print	**3/4 yard**
	(9) 2 1/2" strips cut into (60) triangles
Light Green Print	**2/3 yard**
	(8) 2 5/8" strips cut into (60) half triangle pairs
Medium Green Print	**3/4 yard**
	(9) 2 1/2" strips cut into (60) triangles
Dark Green Print	**3/4 yard**
	(9) 2 1/2" strips cut into (60) triangles
Light Orange Print	**2/3 yard**
	(8) 2 1/2" strips cut into (60) half triangle pairs
Medium Orange Print	**3/4 yard**
	(9) 2 5/8" strips cut into (60) triangles
Dark Orange Print	**3/4 yard**
	(9) 2 1/2" strips cut into (60) triangles
Black Print	**2 1/4 yards**
	(6) 12 1/2" strips for border
Dark Green Solid	**3/4 yard**
	(10) 2 1/4" strips for binding
Backing	**9 yards**

By Carl Hentsch

Other Supplies

Creative Grids CGR120R 120-degree Triangle Strip Ruler

Cutting Triangles

1. Take one of the 2 1/2" strips (several strips may be layered and cut at the same time if preferred) and place the 120-degree triangle ruler on it. The top edge of the ruler should line up with the top of the fabric strip, and the bottom edge of the fabric should match the line marked 2".

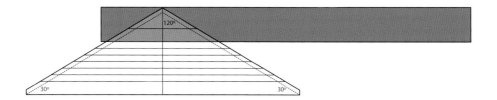

2. Cut both angled sides of the triangle with a rotary cutter.

3. Turn the ruler 180 degrees (do not flip over the ruler) and position it as shown, aligning the cut edge of the fabric with the slanted side of the ruler. Cut along the other slanted edge to make a second triangle.

4. Continue cutting triangles along the length of the strip.

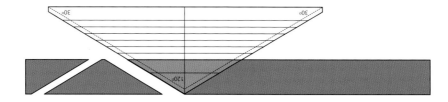

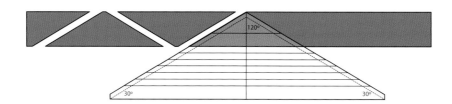

Amish-Inspired
Quilts
for Today's Home

Cutting Half Triangles

To avoid the tricky piecing of three triangles at the center of the design, the third set of strips (the light strips) are cut as two separate halves of a 120-degree triangle.

1. Take two identical light 2 5/8" strips and place them wrong sides together. Cut into 5" rectangles.

2. Place the 120-degree ruler on the 5" piece. Line up the left-hand cut edges of the piece with the left-hand vertical dotted line mark at the center of the ruler.
The lower edge of the fabric should be on the line marked 2. (Fig. 4)

3. Cut along the slanted edge of the ruler through both layers of fabrics.
This will yield a pair of half triangles that are mirror images of each other.
These will be joined to make the third 120-degree triangle in light fabrics for the blocks.

~~~~~~

Block Assembly

Print Fabrics

1. Select six matching light, six matching medium and six matching dark fabrics.
Select each group from a different color way.

2. Arrange two large triangles and two half triangles as shown.
Pin and stitch a half triangle to each of the large triangles, matching seams carefully.
Press the two seams in opposite directions.

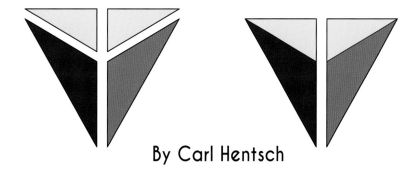

By Carl Hentsch

91

3. Pin and stitch the two halves together, matching seams carefully, to make the large triangle block. Repeat this with the remaining 120-degree triangles and half triangles.

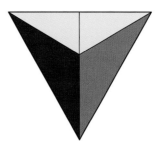

Unfinished size: Each side should measure approximately 7 1/2".
The triangle block will measure approximately 6 1/2" through the center of the block.

4. Make a total of (180) print triangle blocks. Keep each group of six matching triangles in a separate stack for easier assembly of the quilt top.

Black and Gray Fabrics

For the black and gray Triangle Block 1, make **(84)** Black triangles, **(84)** Gray triangles and **(84)** Black half-triangle pairs.

For the gray and black Triangle Block 2, make **(84)** Gray triangles, **(84)** Black triangles and **(84)** Gray half triangle pairs.

1. Arrange the triangles as shown and sew them together, following step 3 in the previous section. Make **84** of each Triangle Block.

Amish-Inspired
Quilts
for Today's Home

Unfinished size: Each side should measure approximately 7 1/2".
The triangle block will measure approximately 6 1/2" through the center of the block.

Half Block Assembly
You will need half blocks to complete the top and bottom of the quilt.

1. Lay out and stitch the half triangles to the triangles as shown in Fig 11. Make the number indicated.

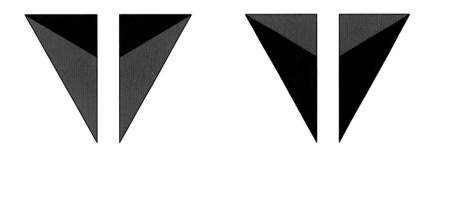

Quilt Assembly

1. Following the layout guide, sew the Triangle Blocks and Half Blocks
into rows, paying attention to the color arrangement. Then sew the rows together.

By Carl Hentsch

Side Borders

1. Sew three 12 1/2" black print border strips together to make one long piece. Repeat with the remaining three border strips.

2. Measure the quilt from top to bottom.

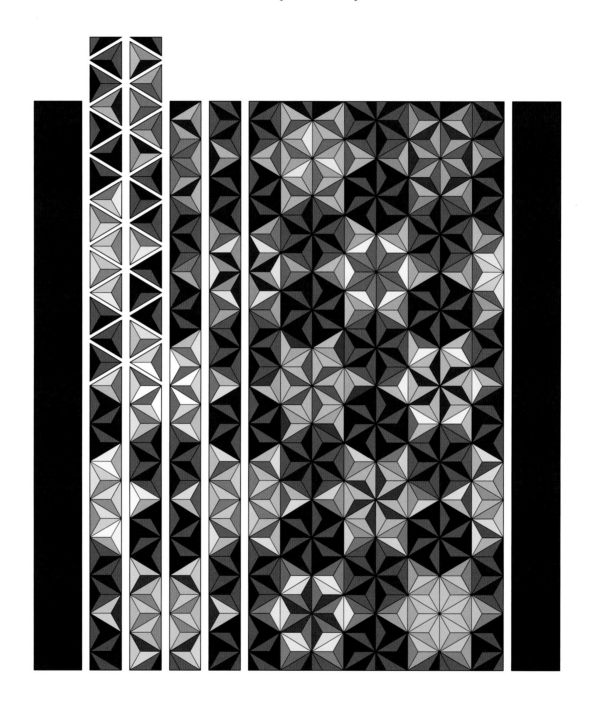

Amish-Inspired
Quilts
for Today's Home

By Carl Hentsch

Finished Quilt

Amish-Inspired
Quilts
for Today's Home